Mom;

I think it [...] help
us if [...] [...]
the day [...] ourselves
and each [...] I think we can:
correction I know we can
get along if we both keep
God on our minds, tongues
and hearts. When you read
our "devotion of the day" don't
forget it right away let
it be stamped in your
mind and reflect upon it
that you may apply to
our life and your relationship
with others. Be good, be happy
but above all have the courage
to be what God would have
you be [...]

Daily Help

Daily Help

Daily Help

By

REV. CHARLES H. SPURGEON

COMPILED AND EDITED BY

GEORGE PERRY DIXON

THE FAMILY INSPIRATIONAL LIBRARY

PUBLISHERS   *Grosset & Dunlap*   NEW YORK

ISBN: 0–448–01637–0
1973 Printing

DAILY HELP

JANUARY 1.

WE will be glad and rejoice in Thee. We will not open the gates of the year to the dolorous notes of the sackbut, but to the sweet strains of the harp of joy. "O come, let us sing unto the Lord: let us make a joyful noise unto the rock of our salvation." What heavens are laid up in Jesus! What rivers of infinite bliss have their source, ay, and every drop of their fullness in Him! Since, O sweet Lord Jesus, Thou art the present portion of Thy people, favor us this year with such a sense of Thy preciousness, that from its first to its last day, we may be glad and rejoice in Thee.

JANUARY 2.

HE who lives without prayer—he who lives with little prayer—he who seldom reads the Word—he who seldom looks up to heaven for a fresh influence from on high—he will be the man whose heart will become dry and barren; but he who calls in secret on his God—who spends much time in holy retirement—who delights to meditate on the words of the Most High—whose soul is given up to Christ—such a man must have an overflowing heart: and as his heart is, such will his life be.

JANUARY 3.

ALL my springs are in thee, and if thou hast all thy springs in God, thy heart will be full enough. If thou dost go to the foot of Calvary, there will thy heart be bathed in love and gratitude. If thou dost frequent the vale of retirement, and there talk with thy God, it is there that thy heart shall be full of calm resolve. If thou goest out with thy master to the hill of Olivet, and dost with him look down upon a wicked Jerusalem, and weep over it with him, then will thy heart be full of love for never-dying souls.

JANUARY 4.

KEEP not back part of the price. Make a full surrender of every motion of thy heart; labor to have but one object and one aim, and for this purpose give God the keeping of thine heart. Cry out for more of the divine influences of the Holy Spirit, so that when thy soul is preserved and protected by Him it may be directed into one channel, and one only, that thy life may run deep and pure, and clear and peaceful; its only banks being God's will, its only channel the love of Christ and a desire to please Him.

JANUARY 5.

*N*EVER, never neglect the word of God; that will make thy heart rich with precept, rich with understanding; and then thy conversation, when it flows from thy mouth, will be like thine heart, rich, unctious and savory. Make thy heart full of rich, generous love, and then the stream that flows from thy hand will be just as rich and generous as thine heart. Oh! go, Christian, to the great mine of riches, and cry unto the Holy Spirit to make thy heart rich unto salvation. So shall thy life and conversation be a boon to thy fellows; and when they see thee, thy face shall be as the angel of God.

JANUARY 6.

*T*HERE is not a spider hanging on the king's wall but hath its errand; there is not a nettle that groweth in the corner of the churchyard but hath its purpose; there is not a single insect fluttering in the breeze but accomplisheth some divine decree; and I will never have it that God created any man, especially any Christian man, to be a blank, and to be a nothing. He made you for an end. Find out what that end is; find out your niche, and fill it. If it be ever so little, if it is only to be a hewer of wood and a drawer of water, do something in this great battle for God and truth.

JANUARY 7.

*S*UPPOSE you see a lake, and there are twenty or thirty streamlets running into it: why, there will not be one strong river in the whole country; there will be a number of little brooks which will be dried up in the summer, and will be temporary torrents in winter. They will every one of them be useless for any great purpose, because there is not water enough in the lake to feed more than one great stream. Now, a man's heart has only enough life in it to pursue one object fully. Ye must not give half your love to Christ, and the other half to the world. No man can serve God and mammon.

JANUARY 8.

*P*RAYER is the rustling of the wings of the angels that are on their way bringing us the boons of heaven. Have you heard prayer in your heart? You shall see the angel in your house. When the chariots that bring us blessings do rumble, their wheels do sound with prayer. We hear the prayer in our own spirits, and that prayer becomes the token of the coming blessings. Even as the cloud foreshadoweth rain, so prayer foreshadoweth the blessing; even as the green blade is the beginning of the harvest, so is prayer the prophecy of the blessing that is about to come.

JANUARY 9.

OMNIPOTENCE may build a thousand worlds, and fill them with bounties; Omnipotence may powder mountains into dust, and burn the sea, and consume the sky, but Omnipotence cannot do an unloving thing toward a believer. Oh! rest quite sure, Christian, a hard thing, an unloving thing from God toward one of his own people is quite impossible. He is as kind to you when he casts you into prison as when he takes you into a palace; He is as good when he sends famine into your house as when he fills your barns with plenty. The only question is, Art thou his child? If so, he hath rebuked thee in affection, and there is love in his chastisement.

JANUARY 10.

DO you not know that God is an eternal self-existent Being; that to say he loves *now*, is, in fact, to say he always did love, since with God there is no past, and can be no future. What we call past, present, and future, he wraps in one eternal NOW. And if you say he loves you now, you say he loved yesterday; he loved in the past eternity; and he will love forever; for *now* with God is past, present, and future.

Christ's love is the sun and our love is the moonlight, which we are able to give forth because the sun hath looked upon us.

JANUARY 11.

*I*F any one should ask me for an epitome of the Christian religion, I should say, it is in that one word—"prayer." If I should be asked, "What will take in the whole of Christian experience?" I should answer, "prayer." A man must have been convinced of sin before he could pray; he must have had some hope that there was mercy for him before he could pray. All the Christian virtues are locked up in the word, prayer.

In troublous times our best communion with God will be carried on by supplication. Tell Him thy case; search out His promise, and then plead it with holy boldness. This is the best, the surest, the speediest way of relief.

JANUARY 12.

*S*INNER, let this be thy comfort, that God sees thee when thou beginnest to repent. He does not see thee with his usual gaze, with which he looks on all men, but he sees thee with an eye of intense interest. He has been looking on thee in all thy sin, and in all thy sorrow, hoping that thou wouldst repent; and now he sees the first gleam of grace, and he beholds it with joy. Never warder on the lonely castle top saw the first gray light of morning with more joy than that with which God beholds the first desire in thy heart.

JANUARY 13.

*A*S sure as God is God, if you this day **are** seeking him aright, through Christ, the day shall come when the kiss of full assurance shall be on your lip, when the arms of sovereign love shall embrace you, and you shall know it to be so. Thou mayest have despised him, but thou shalt know him yet to be thy Father and thy friend. Thou mayest have broken his Sabbaths and despised his Word; the day is coming when the Sabbath shall be thy delight, and his Word thy treasure.

JANUARY 14.

*T*HE great King, immortal, invisible, the Divine person, called the Holy Ghost, the Holy Spirit: it is he that quickens the soul, or else it would lie dead forever; it is he that makes it tender, or else it would never feel; it is he that imparts efficacy to the Word preached, or else it could never reach further than the ear; it is he who breaks the heart, it is he who makes it whole.

There dwells upon this earth a mysterious Being, whose office is to renew the fallen and restore the wandering. We cannot see Him, or hear Him, yet He dwells in some of us as Lord of our nature. His chosen residence is a broken heart and a contrite spirit.

JANUARY 15.

*D*ELIGHT in divine service is a token of acceptance. Those who serve God with a sad countenance, because they do what is unpleasant to them, are not serving Him at all; they bring the form of homage, but the life is absent. That obedience which is not voluntary is disobedience, for the Lord looketh at the heart, and if He seeth that we serve Him from force, and not because we love Him, He will reject our offering. Service coupled with cheerfulness is heart-service, and therefore true. Take away joyful willingness from the Christian, and you have removed *the test of his sincerity.*

Cheerfulness is *the support of our strength;* in the joy of the Lord are we strong.

JANUARY 16.

*T*HE river of God is full of water; but there is not one drop of it that takes its rise in earthly springs. God will have no strength used in his own battles but the strength which he himself imparts; and I would not have you that are now distressed discouraged by it. Your emptiness is but the preparation for your being filled; and your casting down is but the making ready for your lifting up.

Unexpected help shall come to us when affairs are at their worst.

Let us learn from our Master to reckon upon forces invisible.

JANUARY 17.

I GAZE on beauty, and may be myself deformed I admire the light, and may yet dwell in darkness; but if the light of the countenance of God rests upon me, I shall become like unto Him; the lineaments of His visage will be on me, and the great outlines of His attributes will be mine. Oh, wondrous glass, which thus renders the beholder lovely. Oh, admirable mirror, which reflects not self with its imperfections, but gives a perfect image to those that are uncomely.

If thou dost continually draw thine impulse, thy life, the whole of thy being from the Holy Spirit, then shalt thou see God and Jesus face to face.

JANUARY 18.

N OTHING *gives the believer so much joy as fellowship with Christ.* He has enjoyment as others have in the common mercies of life, he can be glad both in God's gifts and God's works; but in all these separately, yea, and in all of them added together, he doth not find such substantial delight as in the matchless person of his Lord Jesus.

Where can such sweetness be found as we have tasted in communion with our Beloved?

If you know anything of the inner life, you will confess that our highest, purest, and most enduring joys must be the fruit of the tree of life which is in the midst of the Paradise of God.

JANUARY 19.

*H*OW encouraging is the thought of the Redeemer's never-ceasing intercession for us. When we pray, He pleads for us; and when we are *not* praying, He is advocating our cause, and by His supplications shielding us from unseen dangers. We little know what we owe to our Saviour's prayers. When we reach the hill-tops of heaven, and look back upon all the way whereby the Lord our God hath led us, how we shall praise Him who, before the eternal throne, has pleaded our cause against our unseen enemies. *"But I have prayed for thee,* that thy faith fail not."

JANUARY 20.

*J*ESUS answered and said, I thank Thee, O Father." It was the habit and life of Jesus to talk with God. May *we* likewise have silent fellowship with the Father, so that often we may answer Him, and though the world wotteth not to whom we speak, may we be responding to that secret voice unheard of any other ear, which our own ear, opened by the Spirit of God, recognizes with joy. What a privilege is intimate communion with the Father of our spirits! It is a secret hidden from the world, a joy with which even the nearest friend intermeddleth not.

This very day may our hearts be in such a state, that when God speaks to us, we, like Jesus, may be prepared at once to *answer* Him.

JANUARY 21.

*B*ELOVED, while we do not neglect external things, which are good enough in themselves, we ought also to see to it that we enjoy living, personal fellowship with Jesus. See to it that sitting at the Saviour's feet is not neglected, even though it be under the specious pretext of doing Him service. The first thing for our soul's health, the first thing for His glory, and the first thing for our own usefulness, is to keep ourselves in perpetual communion with the Lord Jesus, and to see that the vital spirituality of our religion is maintained over and above everything else in the world.

Friendship is one of the sweetest joys of life.

JANUARY 22.

*B*OLDLY come unto the King of kings, from whom no sincere petitioner ever was dismissed unheard.

Whenever there is a heart big with sorrow, wherever there is an eye suffused with tears, wherever there is a lip quivering with agony, wherever there is a deep groan, or a penitential sigh, the ear of Jehovah is wide open. He puts our prayers, like rose leaves, between the pages of His book of remembrance, and when the volume is opened at last, there shall be a precious fragrance springing up therefrom.

JANUARY 23.

*I*T is well to be the sheep of God's pasture, even if we have been wandering sheep. The straying sheep has an owner, and however far it may stray from the fold, it ceases not to belong to that owner. I believe that God will yet bring back into the fold every one of His own sheep, and they shall all be saved. It is something to feel our wanderings, for if we feel ourselves to be lost, we shall certainly be saved; if we feel ourselves to have wandered, we shall certainly be brought back.

JANUARY 24.

*I*F you might go to Heaven and hold communion with some person whom you dearly loved, you would often be found there. But here is Jesus, the King of Heaven, and He gives you that which can open the gates of Heaven and let you in to be with Him, and yet you live without meditating upon His work, meditating upon His person, meditating upon His offices, and meditating upon His glory. Ah! there is nothing that can so console your spirits, and relieve all your distresses and troubles, as the feeling that now you can meditate on the person of Jesus Christ.

JANUARY 25.

*I*N the very beginning, when this great universe lay in the mind of God, like unborn forests in the acorn-cup; long ere the echoes walked the solitudes; before the mountains were brought forth; and long ere the light flashed through the sky, God loved His chosen creatures. Before there was creatureship—when the æther was not fanned by the angel's wing; when space itself had not an existence; when there was nothing save God alone; even then, in that loneliness of Deity, and in that deep quiet and profundity, His love moved for His chosen. Their names were written on His heart, and then were they dear to His soul.

JANUARY 26.

*G*OD is love in its highest degree. He is love rendered more than love. Love is not God, but God is love; He is full of grace, He is the plenitude of mercy—He delighteth in mercy.

I believe that every flower in a garden, which is tended by a wise gardener, could tell of some particular care that the gardener takes of it. He does for the dahlia what he does not for the sunflower; somewhat is wanted by the rose that is not required by the lily; and the geranium calls for an attention which is not given to the honeysuckle. Each flower wins from the gardener a special culture.

He loves us better than we love ourselves.

JANUARY 27.

*H*E who would be happy here must have friends; and he who would be happy hereafter, must above all things, find a friend in the world to come, in the person of God, the Father of His people.

True friendship can only be made between true men. Hearts are the soul of honor. There can be no lasting friendship between bad men. Bad men may pretend to love each other, but their friendship is a rope of sand, which shall be broken at any convenient season; but if a man have a sincere heart within him, and be true and noble, then we may confide in him.

JANUARY 28.

*T*HE imagination will sometimes fly up to God with such a power that eagles' wings cannot match it. It sometimes has such might that it can almost see the King in His beauty, and the land which is very far off. But if it is potent one way, it is another, for imagination has taken us down to the lowest plains of earth. But I rejoice and think of one thing, that I can cry out when this imagination comes upon me. So it is with the Christian. If he cries out, there is hope. Can you chain your imagination? No; but the power of the Holy Ghost can. Ah, it shall do it! and it does do it at last, it does it even on earth.

JANUARY 29.

*T*HE hour is coming, and it may be even now is, when the Holy Ghost shall be poured out again in such a wonderful manner, that many shall run to and fro, and knowledge shall be increased—the knowledge of the Lord shall cover the earth as the waters cover the surface of the great deep; when His kingdom shall come, and His will shall be done on earth even as it is in heaven; when every one will see that verily the Spirit is poured out like water, and the rains are descending from above. For that let us pray; let us continually labor for it, and seek it of God.

JANUARY 30.

*G*OD'S Holy Spirit and man's sin cannot live together peaceably; they may both be in the same heart, but they cannot both reign there, nor can they both be quiet there; for "the Spirit lusteth against the flesh, and the flesh lusteth against the Spirit;" they cannot rest, but there will be a perpetual warring in the soul, so that the Christian will have to cry, "O wretched man that I am! who shall deliver me from the body of this death?" But in due time: the Spirit will drive out all sin, and will present us blameless before the throne of His Majesty with exceeding great joy.

SIMEON called Jesus the consolation of Israel;
and so He was. Before His actual appearance,
His name was the day-star; cheering the darkness,
and prophetic of the rising sun. To Him they
looked with the same hope which cheers the nightly
watcher, when from the lonely castle-top he sees the
fairest of the stars, and hails her as the usher of
the morn. When He was on earth, He must have
been the consolation of all those who were privileged
to be His companions. Like children they would
tell Him of their griefs, and consider Him as their
Father.

FEBRUARY 1.

*O*H! it must have been sweet to have lived with Christ. Surely, sorrows were then but joys in masks, because they gave an opportunity to go to Jesus to have them removed. Oh! would to God, some of us may say, that we could have lain our weary heads upon the bosom of Jesus, and that our birth had been in that happy era, when we might have heard His kind voice, when he said, "Let the weary ones come unto me." But hear how kindly Jesus speaks: "I will not leave you comfortless, for I will pray the Father, and He will send you another Comforter, that He may abide with you forever."

FEBRUARY 2.

*O*UR world has two forces; it has one tendency to run off at a tangent from its orbit; but the sun draws it by a centripetal power, and attracts it to itself. Oh! Christian, thou wilt never walk aright, and keep in the orbit of truth, if it be not for the influence of Christ perpetually attracting thee to the center. Christ is drawing thee to himself, to his likeness, to his character, to his love, to his bosom, and in that way thou art kept from thy natural tendency to fly off and to be lost in the wide fields of sin. Bless God, that Christ lifted up draws all his people unto him.

FEBRUARY 3.

*B*ETTER have two lights than only one. The light of creation is a bright light. God may be seen in the stars; his name is written in gilt letters on the brow of night; you may discover his glory in the ocean waves, yea, in the trees of the field; but it is better to read it in two books than in one. You will find it here more clearly revealed; for he has written this book himself, and he has given you the key to understand it, if you have the Holy Spirit. Ah, beloved, let us thank God for this Bible; let us love it; let us count it more precious than much fine gold.

FEBRUARY 4.

*I*F we had the blessings without asking for them, we should think them common things; but prayer makes the common pebbles of God's temporal bounties more precious than diamonds; and spiritual prayer cuts the diamond, and makes it glisten more.

When thou art wrestling, like Jacob with the angel, and are nearly thrown down, ask the Holy Spirit to nerve thine arm. Consider how the Holy Spirit is the chariot-wheel of prayer. Prayer may be the chariot, the desire may draw it forth, but the Spirit is the very wheel whereby it moveth.

FEBRUARY 5.

*T*HERE are moments when the eyes glisten with joy: and we can say, "we are persuaded, confident, certain." I do not wish to distress anyone who is under doubt. Often gloomy doubts will prevail; there are seasons when you fear you have not been called, when you doubt your interest in Christ. Ah! what a mercy it is that it is not your hold of Christ that saves you, but his hold of you! What a sweet fact that it is not how you grasp his hand, but his grasp of yours, that saves you.

The Lord's promise once given is never recalled.

FEBRUARY 6.

*T*HE gospel is the sum of wisdom; an epitome of knowledge; a treasure-house of truth; and a revelation of mysterious secrets. Our meditation upon it enlarges the mind; and as it opens to our soul in successive flashes of glory, we stand astonished at the profound wisdom manifest in it. Ah, dear friends! if ye seek wisdom, ye shall see it displayed in all its greatness. But turn aside and see this great sight—an incarnate God upon the cross; a substitute atoning for mortal guilt: a sacrifice satisfying the vengeance of Heaven, and delivering the rebellious sinner. Here is essential wisdom; enthroned, crowned, glorified.

FEBRUARY 7.

*D*OST thou know, O saint, how much the Holy Spirit loves thee? Canst thou measure the love of the Spirit? Dost thou know how great is the affection of his soul towards thee? Go measure heaven with thy span; go weigh the mountains in the scales; go take the ocean's water, and tell each drop; go count the sand upon the sea's wide shore; and when thou hast accomplished this, thou canst tell how much he loveth thee. He has loved thee long, he has loved thee well, he loved thee ever, and he still shall love thee; surely he is the person to comfort thee, because he loves.

FEBRUARY 8.

*S*OME persons say they cannot bear to be an hour in solitude; they have got nothing to do, nothing to think about. No Christian will ever talk so, surely; for if I can but give him one word to think of—Christ—let him spell that over forever; let me give him the word Jesus, and only let him try to think it over, and he shall find that an hour is naught, and that eternity is not half enough to utter our glorious Saviour's praise.

From a sweet fountain of thought we shall have sweet waters of talk. It is sweet to live in the thoughts of those we love.

FEBRUARY 9.

*T*HE canon revelation is closed; there is no more to be added; God does not give a fresh revelation, but he rivets the old one. When it has been forgotten, and laid in the dusty chamber of our memory, he brings it forth and cleans the picture, but does not paint a new one. It is not by any new revelation that the Spirit comforts. He does so by telling us old things over again; he brings a fresh lamp to manifest the treasures hidden in Scripture; he unlocks the strong chests in which the truth has long lain, and he points to secret chambers filled with untold riches; but he coins no more, for enough is done.

FEBRUARY 10.

*M*OST of the grand truths of God have to be learned by trouble; they must be burned into us with the hot iron of affliction, otherwise we shall not truly receive them. No man is competent to judge in matters of the kingdom, until first he has been tried; since there are many things to be learned in the depths which we can never know in the heights. He shall best meet the wants of God's people who has had those wants himself; he shall best comfort God's Israel who has needed comfort; and he shall best preach salvation who has felt his own need of it.

FEBRUARY 11.

*I*F I desired to put myself in the most likely place for the Lord to meet with me, I should prefer the house of prayer, for it is in preaching, that the Word is most blessed; but still I think I should equally desire the reading of the Scriptures; for I might pause over every verse, and say, "Such a verse was blessed to so many souls; then, why not to me? I am at least in the pool of Bethesda; I am walking amongst its porches, and who can tell but that the angel will stir the pool of the Word, whilst I lie helplessly by the side of it, waiting for the blessing?"

FEBRUARY 12.

*O*H! it is a happy way of smoothing sorrow when we can say, "We will wait only upon God." Oh, ye agitated Christians, do not dishonor your religion by always wearing a brow of care; come, cast your burden up on the Lord. I see ye staggering beneath a weight which He would not feel. What seems to you a crushing burden, would be to him but as the small dust of the balance. See! the Almighty bends his shoulders, and he says, "Here, put thy troubles here."

"Come unto Me, and I will give you rest."

FEBRUARY 13.

CHRIST is the chariot in which souls are drawn to heaven. The people of the Lord are on their way to heaven; they are carried in everlasting arms; and those arms are the arms of Christ. Christ is carrying them up to his own house, to his own throne; by-and-by his prayer, "Father, I will that they whom thou hast given me be with me where I am," shall be wholly fulfilled. The cross is the great covenant transport which will weather out the storms, and reach its desired heaven. This is the chariot, the pillars wherewith are of gold; it is lined with the purple of the atonement of our Lord Jesus Christ.

FEBRUARY 14.

WHAT! is Christ thy Brother, and does he live in thine house, and yet thou hast not spoken to him for a month? I fear there is little love between thee and thy Brother, for thou hast had no conversation with him for so long. What! is Christ the Husband of his Church, and has she had no fellowship with him for all this time?

Prayer is the outcome of that sense of need which arises from the new life; a man would not pray to God if he did not feel that he had urgent need of blessings which only the Lord can bestow.

Prayer is the autograph of the Holy Ghost upon the renewed heart.

FEBRUARY 15.

*T*O know one's self to be foolish is to stand upon the door-step of the temple of wisdom; to understand the wrongness of any position is half way towards amending it; to be quite sure that our self-confidence is sin and folly, and an offense towards God, is a great help towards the absolute casting of our self-confidence away, and the bringing of our souls, in practice as well as in theory, to rely wholly upon the power of God's Holy Spirit.

Nobody will err about the way to God if he really resolves to follow that way. The Spirit of God will guide those whose hearts are set upon coming to God.

FEBRUARY 16.

*Y*OU cannot, though you may think you can, preserve a moderation in sin. If you commit one sin, it is like the melting of the lower glacier upon the Alps; the others must follow in time. As certainly as you heap one stone upon the cairn to-day, the next day you will cast another, until the heap, reared stone by stone, shall become a very pyramid. Set the coral insect at work, you cannot decree where it shall stay its work. It will not build its rock just as high as you please; it will not stay until there shall be soil upon it, and an island shall be created by tiny creatures. Sin cannot be held in with bit and bridle.

FEBRUARY 17.

*F*ROM the cross of Calvary, where the bleeding hands of Jesus drop mercy; from the garden of Gethsemane, the cry comes, "Look unto me, and be saved, all the ends of the earth." From Calvary's summit, where Jesus cries, "It is finished," I hear a shout, "Look, and be saved." But there comes a cry from our soul, "Nay, look to yourself!" Ah, look to yourself, and you will be lost. As long as you look to yourself there is no hope for you. It is not a consideration of what you are, but a consideration of what God is, and what Christ is, that can save you.

FEBRUARY 18.

*I*F you know these two things—yourself a sinner and Christ a Saviour it is looking from yourself to Jesus. Oh! there be men that quite misunderstand the gospel; they think that righteousness qualifies them to come to Christ; whereas sin is the only qualification for a man to come to Jesus. Good old Crisp says, "Righteousness keeps me from Christ: the whole have no need of a physician, but they that are sick. Sin makes me come to Jesus, when sin is felt; and in coming to Christ, the more sin I have the more cause I have to hope for mercy."

FEBRUARY 19.

*A*S a man does not make himself spiritually alive, so neither can he keep himself so. He can feed on spiritual food, and so preserve his spiritual strength; he can walk in the commandments of the Lord, and so enjoy rest and peace, but still the inner life is dependent upon the Spirit as much for its after existence as for its first begetting. No man himself, even when converted, hath any power, except as that power is daily, constantly, and perpetually infused into him by the Spirit.

The motive-power of action to a believing man lies hard by the realization that God, for Christ's sake, hath forgiven his iniquities.

FEBRUARY 20.

*C*ULTIVATE a cheerful disposition; endeavor, as much as lieth in you, always to bear a smile about with you; recollect that this is as much a command of God as that one which says, "Thou shalt love the Lord with all thy heart."

Let us take the pure gold of thankfulness and the jewels of praise and make them into another crown for the head of Jesus.

When it is the Lord's work in which we rejoice, we need not be afraid of being too glad.

Cheerfulness is most becoming in Christian men.

Contentment is the crown jewel of a happy life.

FEBRUARY 21.

*Y*OU may think of a doctrine forever, and get no good from it, if you are not already saved; but think of the person of Christ, and that will give you faith. Take him everywhere, wherever you go, and try to meditate on him in your leisure moments, and then he will reveal himself to you, and give you peace.

We should all know more, live nearer to God and grow in grace, if we were more alone. Meditation chews the cud and extracts the real nutriment from the mental food gathered elsewhere.

Read the Bible carefully, and then meditate and meditate and meditate.

FEBRUARY 22.

*T*HERE is no loss in being a Christian, and making God the first object; but make anything else your goal, and with all your running, should you run ever so well, you shall fall short of the mark; or if you gain it, you shall fall uncrowned, unhonored to the earth. "My soul, wait thou only upon God."

He that serves God in body, soul, and spirit, to the utmost of his power, finds new power given to him hour by hour, for God opens to him fresh springs.

The ideal Christian is one who has been made alive with a life which he lives for God.

FEBRUARY 23.

*T*HE book of nature is an expression of the thoughts of God. We have God's terrible thoughts in the thunder and lightning; God's loving thoughts in the sunshine and the balmy breeze; God's bounteous, prudent, careful thoughts in the waving harvest and in the ripening meadow. We have God's brilliant thoughts in the wondrous scenes which are beheld from mountain-top and valley; and we have God's most sweet and pleasant thoughts of beauty in the little flowers that blossom at our feet. "God giveth us richly all things to enjoy."

FEBRUARY 24.

*I*T may be, that during a sermon two men are listening to the same truth; one of them hears as attentively as the other, and remembers as much of it; the other is melted to tears or moved with solemn thoughts; but the one though equally attentive, sees nothing in the sermon, except, may be, certain important truths well set forth; as for the other, his heart is broken within him and his soul is melted. Ask me how it is that the same truth has an effect upon this one, and not upon the other: because the mysterious Spirit of the living God goes with the truth to one heart and not to the other.

FEBRUARY 25.

THERE are some that are like what is fabled of the swan. The ancients said that the swan never sang in his lifetime, but always sang just when he died. Now, there are many of God's desponding children, who seem to go all their life under a cloud; but they get a swan's song before they die. The river of their life comes running down, perhaps black and miry with troubles, and when it begins to touch the white foam of the sea there comes a little glistening in its waters. So, beloved, though we may have been very much dispirited by reason of the burden of the way, when we get to the end we shall have sweet songs.

FEBRUARY 26.

IT is marvelous that the men who most of all rail at faith, are remarkable for credulity. Not caring to have God in their hearts, forsaking the living fountain, they have hewn out to themselves cisterns which are broken, and hold no water. Oh, that we may each of us be more wise, that we may not forsake the good old path, nor leave the way that God hath prepared for us. What wonder we should travel amongst thorns and briars, and rend our own flesh, or worse than that, fall among dark mountains, and be lost among the chasms thereof, if we despise the guidance of our unerring Father.

FEBRUARY 27.

*B*EHOLD, him whom thou canst not behold! Lift up thine eyes to heaven and see ye him, who stretched the heavens like a tent to dwell in, and then did weave into their tapestry, with golden needle, stars that glitter in the darkness. Mark ye him who spread the earth, and created man upon it. He is all-sufficient, eternal, self-existent, unchangeable! Wilt thou not reverence him? He is good, he is loving, he is kind, he is gracious! See the bounties of his providence; behold the plenitude of his grace! Wilt thou not love Jehovah, because he is Jehovah?

FEBRUARY 28.

*O*H! ye kind and affectionate hearts, who are not rich in wealth, but who are rich in love—and that is the world's best wealth—put this golden coin among your silver ones, and it will sanctify them.

The love of Christ casts not out the love of relatives, but it sanctifies our loves, and makes them sweeter far. Remember the love of men and women is very sweet. Oh! to have the love of Christ! for his love is "strong as death and mightier than the grave."

The most overpowering thought of all is that He loved us when there was nothing good in us whatever.

MARCH 1.

HEAVEN is a place of complete victory and triumph. This is the battle-field; there is the triumphal procession. This is the land of the sword and the spear; that is the land of the wreath and the crown. Oh, what a thrill of joy shall shoot through the hearts of all the blessed when their conquests shall be complete in heaven, when death itself, the last of foes, shall be slain—when Satan shall be dragged captive at the chariot wheels of Christ—when he shall have overthrown sin—when the great shout of universal victory shall rise from the hearts of all the redeemed!

MARCH 2.

SALVATION is God's highest glory. He is glorified in every dewdrop that twinkles to the morning sun. He is magnified in every wood flower that blossoms in the copse, although it live to blush unseen and waste its sweetness in the forest air. But sing, sing, O Universe, till thou hast exhausted thyself, thou canst not afford a song so sweet as the song of Incarnation. There is more in that than in creation, more melody in Jesus in the manger, than there is in worlds on worlds rolling their grandeur round the throne of the Most High.

MARCH 3.

*T*HE saints in Jesus, when their bodies sleep in peace, have perpetual fellowship with him—ay, better fellowship than we can enjoy. We have but the transitory glimpse of his face; they gaze upon it every moment. We see him "in a glass, darkly;" they behold him "face to face." We sip of the brook by the way; they plunge into the very ocean of unbounded love. We look up sometimes, and see our Father smile; look whenever they may, his face is always full of smiles for them. We get some drops of comfort, but they get the honeycomb itself. They are full of peace, full of joy for ever. They "sleep in Jesus."

MARCH 4.

*T*HIS city of refuge had round it suburbs of a very great extent. Two thousand cubits were allowed for grazing land for the cattle of the priests, and a thousand cubits within these for fields and vineyards. Now, no sooner did the man reach the outside of the city, the suburbs, than he was safe; it was not necessary for him to get within the walls, but the suburbs themselves were sufficient protection. Learn, hence, that if ye do but touch the hem of Christ's garment, ye shall be made whole; if ye do but lay hold of him with "faith as a grain of mustard seed," with faith which is scarcely a believing, but is truly a believing, you are safe.

MARCH 5.

*B*EHOLD the unpillared arch of heaven; see how it stretches its gigantic span; and yet it falleth not, though it is unpropped and unbuttressed. "He hangeth the world upon nothing." What chain is it that bindeth up the stars, and keepeth them from falling? A Christian should be a second exhibition of God's universe; his faith should be an unpillared confidence, resting on the past, and on the eternity to come, as the sure groundwork of its arch. His faith should be like the world, it should hang on nothing but the promise of God, needing nothing to uphold him but the right hand of his Father.

MARCH 6.

*O*H! how did heaven wonder! how did the stars stand still with astonishment! and how did the angels stay their songs a moment, when for the first time, God showed how he might be just, and yet be gracious! Oh! sinner, my heart hath devised it; my Son, the pure and perfect, shall stand in thy stead, and be accounted guilty, and thou, the guilty, shalt stand in my Son's stead and be accounted righteous!" It would make us leap upon our feet in astonishment if we did but understand this thoroughly—the wonderful mystery of the transposition of Christ and the sinner.

MARCH 7.

*I*F little things have done great things, let us try to do great things also. You know not, ye atoms, but that your destiny is sublime. Try and make it so by faith; and the least of you may be mighty through the strength of God. Oh, for grace to trust God, and there is no telling what ye can do. Spirit of the living God! we want thee. Thou art the life, the soul, thou art the source of thy people's success; without thee they can do nothing, with thee they can do everything. "It is not by armies, nor by power but by my Spirit, saith the Lord."

MARCH 8.

*O*H! who shall measure the heights of the Saviour's all-sufficiency? First, tell how high is sin, and, then, remember that as Noah's flood prevailed over the tops of earth's mountains, so the flood of Christ's redemption prevails over the tops of the mountains of our sins. In heaven's courts there are to-day men that once were sinners, but they have been washed—they have been sanctified. Ask them whence the brightness of their robes hath come, and where their purity hath been achieved, and they, with united breath, tell you that they have washed their robes, and made them white in the blood of the Lamb.

MARCH 9.

*I*T will not save me to know that Christ is a Saviour; but it will save me *to trust* him to be *my* Saviour. I shall not be delivered from the wrath to come, by believing that his atonement is sufficient; but I shall be saved by making that atonement my trust, my refuge, and my all. The pith, the essence of faith lies in this—a casting oneself on the promise. It is not the life buoy on board ship that saves the man when he is drowning, nor is it his belief that it is an excellent and successful invention. No! he must have it around his loins, or his hand upon it, or else he will sink.

MARCH 10.

*Y*OU see yonder ship. After a long voyage, it has neared the haven, but is much injured; the sails are rent to ribbons. That is like the righteous being "scarcely saved." But do you see that other ship? It has made a prosperous voyage; and now, laden to the water's edge, with the sails all up and with the white canvas filled with the wind, it rides into the harbor joyously and nobly. That is an "abundant entrance;" and if you and I are helped by God's Spirit to add to our faith, virtue, and so on, we shall have at the last an "abundant entrance into the kingdom of our Lord Jesus Christ."

MARCH 11.

*D*EAR friends, the last song in this world, the song of triumph, shall be full of God, and of no one else. Here you praise the instrument; to-day you look on this man and on that, and you say, "Thank God for this minister, and for this man!" But in that day, forgotten shall their names be for a season, even as the stars refuse to shine when the sun himself appeareth. The song shall be unto Jehovah, and Jehovah only; "Unto him that loved us, and hath washed us from our sins in his own blood, unto him be glory forever and ever. Amen."

MARCH 12.

*W*HEN no eye seeth you except the eye of God, when darkness covers you, when you are shut up from the observation of mortals, even then be ye like Jesus Christ. Remember his ardent piety, his secret devotion—how, after laboriously preaching the whole day, he stole away in the midnight shades to cry for help from his God. Recollect how his entire life was constantly sustained by fresh inspirations of the Holy Spirit, derived by prayer. Take care of your secret life: let it be such that you will not be ashamed to read at the last great day.

MARCH 13.

*T*HE death of the saints is precious in the sight of the Lord. On their account we have cause rather to rejoice than to weep. Yes, we have the fond and firm persuasion that already their redeemed spirits have flown up to the eternal throne. We do believe that they are at this moment joining in the hallelujahs of paradise, feasting on the fruits of the tree of life, and walking by the side of the "river, the streams whereof make glad the heavenly city of our God." We know they are supremely blest; we think of them as glorified spirits above, who are present with the Lord Jesus.

MARCH 14.

*Y*E have lost your friends some of you, come to the grave of your best friend—your brother, yea, one who "sticketh closer than a brother." Come thou to the grave of thy dearest relative, O Christian, for Jesus is thy husband. "Thy maker is thy husband, the Lord of Hosts is his name." Doth not affection draw you? Do not the sweet lips of love woo you? Is not the place sanctified where one so well beloved slept, although but for a moment? Surely ye need no eloquence. I have but the power, in simple, but earnest accents, to repeat the words. "Come, see the place where the Lord lay."

MARCH 15.

OH!" cries one, "I wish I could escape the wrath of the law! Oh that I knew that Christ did keep the law for me!" Stop, then, and I will tell you. Do you feel to-day that you are guilty, lost, and ruined? Do you, with tears in your eyes, confess that none but Jesus can do you good? Are you willing to give up all trusts, and cast yourself alone on him who died upon the cross? Can you look to Calvary, and see the bleeding sufferer, all crimson with streams of gore? Then he kept the law for you, and the law cannot condemn whom Christ has absolved.

MARCH 16.

THE Bible is a vein of pure gold, unalloyed by quartz, or any earthly substance. This is a star without a speck; a sun without a blot; a light without darkness; a moon without its paleness; a glory without a dimness. O Bible! it cannot be said of any other book, that it is perfect and pure; but of thee we can declare all wisdom is gathered up in thee, without a particle of folly. This is the judge that ends the strife, where wit and reason fail. This is the book untainted by any error; but is pure, unalloyed, perfect truth.

MARCH 17.

*P*OOR sinner, do take heart, remember God knows, as we know not, where thou art. If thou art in the deepest pit in the forest, his almighty eye can see to the bottom. Ay, and in one of the favored moments of the day of salvation—that time accepted—he will send home a promise so sweetly that all thy fetters shall break off in an instant—thy night shall be scattered—thy dawn begin; and he will give thee the oil of joy for mourning and the garment of praise for the spirit of heaviness. Believe now, and thou shalt be comforted now; for the time of faith is the time of comfort.

MARCH 18.

*N*O inferior hand hath sketched even so much as the most minute parts of providence. It was all marked out, designed, and planned by the mind of the all-wise, all-knowing God. Hence, not even Christ's death was exempt from it. He that wings an angel and guides a sparrow, he that counts the hairs of our head, was not likely, when he took notice of such little things, to omit the greatest wonder of earth's miracles, the death of Christ. No; the blood-stained page of that book, the page which makes both past and future glorious with golden words—that blood-stained page, I say, was as much written of Jehovah as any other.

MARCH 19.

*M*AN cannot please God without bringing himself a great amount of happiness; for if any man pleases God, it is because God accepts him as his son, gives him the blessings of adoption, pours upon him the bounties of his grace, makes him a blessed man in this life, and insures him a crown of everlasting life, which he shall wear, and which shall shine with unfading luster, when the wreaths of earth's glory have all been melted away; while, on the other hand, if a man does not please God, he inevitably brings upon himself sorrow and suffering in this life.

MARCH 20.

*C*HRIST is the same; Christ's person never changes. Should he come on earth to visit us again, as sure he will, we should find him the same Jesus; as loving, as approachable, as generous, as kind, and though arrayed in nobler garments than he wore when first he visited earth, though no more the Man of Sorrows and grief's acquaintance, yet he would be the same person, unchanged by all his glories, his triumphs, and his joys. We bless Christ that amid his heavenly splendors his person is just the same, and his nature unaffected. "Jesus Christ the same yesterday, and to-day, and forever."

MARCH 21.

*B*UT two opinions in the matter of soul-religion you cannot hold. If God be God, serve him, and do it thoroughly; but if this world be God, serve it, and make no profession of religion. If you think the things of the world the best, serve them. But remember, if the Lord be your God, you cannot have Baal too; you must have one thing or else the other. "No man can serve two *masters*." If God be served, he will be a master; and if the devil be served, he will not be long before he will be a master; and "ye cannot serve two *masters*." Oh! be wise, and think not that the two can be mingled together.

MARCH 22.

*D*ID you ever think of the love which Christ will manifest to you, when he shall present you without spot, or blemish, or any such thing, before his Father's throne? Well, pause and remember, that he loves you at this hour as much as he will love you then; for he will be the same forever as he is to-day, and he is the same to-day as he will be forever. "As the Father hath loved me, even so have I loved you;" and a higher degree of love we cannot imagine. The Father loves his Son infinitely, and even so to-day, believer, doth the Son of God love thee.

MARCH 23.

O CHILDREN of God! death hath lost its sting. It is sweet to die; to lie upon the breast of Christ, and have one's soul kissed out of one's body by the lips of divine affection. And you that have lost friends, or that may be bereaved, sorrow not as those who are without hope. What a sweet thought the death of Christ brings us concerning those who are departed! They are gone, my brethren; but do you know how far they have gone? The distance between the glorified spirits in heaven and the militant saints on earth seems great; but it is not so. We are not far from home.

MARCH 24.

T HERE is one great event, which every day attracts more admiration than do the sun, and moon, and stars. That event is the death of our Lord Jesus Christ. To it the eyes of all the saints who lived before the Christian era were always directed; and backwards, through the thousand years of history, the eyes of all modern saints are looking. Upon Christ, the angels in heaven perpetually gaze. "Which things the angels desire to look into," said the apostle. Upon Christ, the eyes of the redeemed are perpetually fixed; and thousands of pilgrims, through this world of tears, have no higher object for their faith.

MARCH 25.

YOU have sometimes seen how the ship cuts through the billows, leaving a white furrow behind her, and causing the sea to boil around her. Such is life, says Job, "like the swift ships." I cannot stop its motion; I may direct it with the rudder of God's Holy Spirit; but nevertheless, like a swift ship, my life must speed on its way until it reaches its haven. Where is that haven to be? Shall it be found in the land of bitterness and barrenness, that dreary region of the lost? Or shall it be that sweet haven of eternal peace?

MARCH 26.

THE holiest men, the most free from *impurity*, have always felt it most. He whose garments are the whitest, will best perceive the spots upon them. He whose crown shineth the brightest, will know when he hath lost a jewel. He who giveth the most light to the world, will always be able to discover his own darkness. The angels of heaven veil their faces; and the angels of God on earth, his chosen people, must always veil their faces with humility, when they think of what they were.

As you grow *downward* in humility seek also to grow *upward*, having nearer approaches to God in prayer and more intimate fellowship with Jesus.

MARCH 27.

*O*H! there is nothing that can so advantage you, nothing can so prosper you, so assist you, so make you walk towards heaven rapidly, so keep your head upwards towards the sky, and your eyes radiant with glory, like the imitation of Jesus Christ. It is when, by the power of the Holy Spirit, you are enabled to walk with Jesus in his very footsteps, and tread in his ways, you are most happy and you are most known to be the sons of God. For your sake, my brethren, I say, be like Christ.

To draw him nearer to me, and myself nearer to him, is the innermost longing of my soul.

MARCH 28.

*H*E that loveth much must weep much; much love and much sorrow must go together in this vale of tears. Oftimes tears are the index of strength. There are periods when they are the noblest thing in the world. The tears of penitents are precious; a cup of them were worth a king's ransom. It is no sign of weakness when a man weeps for sin; it shows that he hath strength of mind; nay, more, that he hath strength imparted by God, which enables him to forswear his lusts and overcome his passions, and to turn unto God with full purpose of heart.

MARCH 29.

O MY heart, I bid thee now put thy treasure where thou canst never lose it. Put it in Christ; put all thine affections in his person, all thy hope in his glory, all thy trust in his efficatious blood, all thy joy in his presence, and then thou wilt have put thyself and put thine all where thou canst never lose anything, because it is secure. Go, tell thy secrets to that friend that sticketh closer than a brother. My heart, I charge thee, trust all thy concerns with him who never can be taken from thee, who will never let thee leave him, even "Jesus Christ the same yesterday, and to-day, and forever."

MARCH 30.

*I*F any of your desire to be saved by works, remember one sin will spoil your righteousness; one dust of this earth's dross will spoil the beauty of that perfect righteousness which God requires at your hands. If ye would be saved by works, ye must be as holy as the angels, ye must be as pure and as immaculate as Jesus; for the law requires perfection.

The power to receive is scarcely a power, and yet it is the only power needed for salvation. Come along and take what Christ doth freely give you.

Believe in the Lord Jesus Christ, and believe intensely.

MARCH 31.

*T*HOSE who have not to work hard, think they will love heaven as a place of service. That is very true. But to the working man, to the man who toils with his brain or with his hands, it must ever be a sweet thought that there is a land where we shall rest. Oh! weary sons and daughters of Adam, ye shall be still, ye shall be quiet, ye shall rest yourselves, for all are rich in heaven, all are happy there, all are peaceful. Toil, trouble, travail, and labor, are words that cannot be spelled in heaven; they have no such things there, for they always rest.

APRIL 1.

"COME, see the place where the Lord lay." Surely ye need no argument to move your feet in the direction of the holy sepulcher; but still we will use the utmost power to draw your spirit thither. Ask me the greatest man who ever lived—I tell you the man Christ Jesus was "anointed with the oil of gladness above his fellows." If ye seek a chamber honored as the resting-place of Jesus, turn in hither; if ye would worship at the grave of holiness, come ye here; if ye would see the hallowed spot, come with me, Christian, to that quiet garden, hard by the walls of Jerusalem.

APRIL 2.

COMING to Christ is just the one essential thing for a sinner's salvation. He that cometh not to Christ is yet in "the gall of bitterness and in the bonds of iniquity." Coming to Christ is the very first effect of regeneration. No sooner is the soul quickened than it at once discovers its lost estate, looks out for a refuge, and believing Christ to be the only one, flies to him and reposes in him. Where there is not this coming to Christ, it is certain that there is as yet no quickening; where there is no quickening, the soul is dead in trespass and sins, and being dead it cannot enter into the kingdom of heaven.

APRIL 3.

SINNER, unconverted sinner, thou hast often tried to save thyself; but thou hast often failed. Thou hast, by thine own power and might, sought to curb thy evil passions and sins; with thee, I lament that all thine efforts have been unsuccessful. And I warn thee, it will be unsuccessful, for thou never canst by thine own might save thyself; with all the strength thou hast, thou never canst regenerate thine own soul; thou canst never cause thyself to be born again. And though the new birth is absolutely necessary, it is absolutely impossible to thee, unless God the Spirit shall do it.

APRIL 4.

PRAYER is the certain forerunner of salvation. Sinner, thou canst not pray and perish; prayer and perishing are two things that never go together. I ask you not what your prayer is; it may be a groan, it may be a tear, but if it be a prayer from the inmost heart thou shalt be saved; yet if from thine heart thou hast learned to pray—

"Prayer is the breath of God in man,
Returning whence it came"—

And thou canst not perish with God's breath in thee. "Whosoever shall call upon the name of the Lord shall be saved!"

APRIL 5.

$\mathcal{L}$ ET not your exertions end in tears, mere weeping will do nothing without action. Get on your feet; ye that have voices and might, go forth and preach the gospel, preach it in every street and lane of this huge city; ye that have wealth, go forth and spend it for the poor, and sick, and needy, and dying, the uneducated, the unenlightened; ye that have time, go forth and spend it in deeds of goodness; ye that have power in prayer go forth and pray;—every one to his post, every one of you to your gun in this day of battle; now for God and for his truth; for God and for the right; let every one of us who knows the Lord seek to fight under his banner!

APRIL 6.

$\mathcal{B}$Y the sweet drawing of the Spirit, the sinner finds "a peace with God which passeth all understanding, which keeps his heart and mind through Jesus Christ our Lord." Now, you will plainly perceive that all this may be done without any compulsion. Man is as much drawn willingly, as if he were not drawn at all; and he comes to Christ with full consent, with as full a consent as if no secret influence had ever been exercised in his heart. But that influence must be exercised, or else there never has been and there never will be, any man who either can or will come to the Lord Jesus Christ

APRIL 7.

I WILL *help* thee. That is very little for me to do, to *help* thee. Consider what I have done already. What! not help thee? Why, I bought thee with my blood. What! not help thee? I have died for thee; and if I have done the greater, will I not do the less? *Help* thee, my beloved! It is the least thing I will ever do for thee. I have done more, and I will do more. Before the day-star first began to shine I chose thee. "I will *help* thee." I made the covenant for thee, and exercised all the wisdom of my eternal mind in the plan of salvation. "I will *help* thee."

APRIL 8.

*C*HRIST longed for the cross, because he looked for it as the goal of all his exertions. He could never say "It is finished" on his throne: but on his cross he did cry it. He preferred the sufferings of Calvary to the honors of the multitude who crowded round about him; for bless and heal them as he might, still was his work undone. "I long for my sufferings, because they shall be the completion of my great work of grace." It is the end that bringeth the honor; it is the victory that crowneth the warrior rather than the battle. And so Christ longed for this, his death, that he might see the completion of his labor.

APRIL 9.

*C*AN ye think what must have been the greatness of the atonement which was the substitution for all this agony which God would have cast upon us, if he had not poured it upon Christ?

And can you grasp the thought of the greatness of your Saviour's mediation when he paid your debt, and paid it all at once; so that there now remaineth not one farthing of debt owing from Christ's people to their God, except a debt of love. Christ did pay it all, so that man is set free from all punishment, through what Jesus hath done. Think ye, then, how great his atonement if he hath done all this.

APRIL 10.

*T*HE old saying is, "Go from nature up to nature's God;" but it is hard working up hill. The best thing is to go from nature's God down to nature; and, if you once get to nature's God, and believe Him, and love Him, it is surprising how easy it is to hear music in the waves, and songs in the wild whisperings of the winds; to see God everywhere, in the stones, in the rocks, in the rippling brooks, and hear him everywhere in the lowing of cattle, in the rolling of thunders, and in the fury of tempests. Get Christ first, put him in the right place, and you will find him to be the wisdom of God in your own experience.

APRIL 11.

*W*HEREVER the church is, there is God. God is pleased, in his mercy and condescension, to stoop from the highest heavens to dwell in this lower heaven—the heaven of his church. It is here, among the household of faith, he deigns—let me say it with sacred reverence—to unbend himself, and hold familiar intercourse with those round about him whom he hath adopted into his family. He may be a consuming fire abroad, but when he comes into his own house he is all mercy, mildness, and love. Abroad he does great works of power; but at home in his own house he does great works of grace.

APRIL 12.

*M*ANY men believe in the existence of a God, but they do not love that belief. But to the Christian the thought that there is a God is the sunshine of his existence. His intellect bows before the Most High; like the angel who prostrates himself because he loves to adore his Maker. His intellect is as fond of God as his imagination. "Oh!" he saith, "my God, I bless thee that thou art; for thou art my highest treasure, my richest and my rarest delight. I love thee with all my intellect; I have neither thought nor judgment, nor conviction, nor reason, which I do not lay at thy feet, and consecrate to thine honor."

APRIL 13.

*E*ACH of God's saints is sent into the world to prove some part of the divine character. In heaven we shall read the great book of the experience of all the saints, and gather from that book the whole of the divine character as having been proved and illustrated. Each Christian man is a manifestation and display of some position or other of God; a different part may belong to each of us, but when the whole shall be combined, when all the rays of evidence shall be brought, as it were, into one great sun, and shine forth with meridian splendor, we shall see in Christian experience a beautiful revelation of our God.

APRIL 14.

*I*F I once wandered on yon mountain top, and Jesus climbed up and caught me, and put me on his shoulders, and carried me home, I cannot and dare not doubt that He is my Shepherd. If I had belonged to some other sheep owner, he would not have sought me. And from the fact that He did seek, I learn that He must be my Shepherd. Could I trace my deliverance to the hand of a creature, I should think that some creature might be my shepherd; but since he who has been reclaimed of God must confess that God alone has done it, such a one will feel persuaded that the Lord must be his Shepherd, because He brought him, He delivered him.

APRIL 15.

*A*H! if we did but love Christ better, my brothers and sisters, if we lived nearer to the cross, if we knew more of the value of his blood, if we wept like him over Jerusalem, if we felt more what it was for souls to perish, and what it was for men to be saved,—if we did but rejoice with Christ in the prospect of his seeing the travail of his soul, and being abundantly satisfied,—if we did but delight more in the divine decree, that the kingdoms of this world *shall* be given to Christ, I am sure we should all of us find more ways and more means for the sending forth of the gospel of Christ.

APRIL 16.

*H*EAVEN singeth evermore. Before the throne of God angels and redeemed saints extol his name. And this world is singing too; sometimes with the loud noise of the rolling thunder, of the boiling sea, of the dashing cataract, and of the lowing cattle; and often with that still, solemn harmony which floweth from the vast creation, when in its silence it praiseth God.

In heaven they sing, "The Lord be exalted; let his name be magnified forever." And the earth singeth the same: "Great art thou in thy works, O Lord! and unto thee be glory."

APRIL 17.

*L*OVE to Christ smooths the path of duty, and wings the feet to travel it: it makes the life of sincere devotion.

Love has a clear eye; but it can see only one thing, —it is blind to every interest but that of its Lord; it seeth things in the light of his glory, and weigheth actions in the scales of his honor; it counts royalty but drudgery if it cannot reign for Christ, but it delights in servitude as much as in honor, if it can thereby advance the Master's kingdom; its end sweetens all its means; its object lightens its toil, and removes its weariness.

APRIL 18.

*I*N nature, after evening time there cometh night. The sun hath had its hour of journeying; the fiery steeds are weary; they must rest. Lo, they descend the azure steeps and plunge their burning fetlocks in the western sea, while night in her ebon chariot follows at their heels. God, however, oversteps the rule of nature. He is pleased to send to his people times when the eye of reason expects to see no more day, but fears that the glorious landscape of God's mercies will be shrouded in the darkness of his forgetfulness. But instead thereof, God overleapeth nature, and declares that at evening time, instead of darkness, there shall be light.

APRIL 19.

*W*HEN Jesus Christ came to build his temple, he found no mountain on which to build it; he had no mountain in our nature, he had to find a mountain in his own, and the mountain upon which he has built his Church is the mountain of his own unchangeable affection, his own strong love, his own omnipotent grace and infallible truthfulness. It is this that constitutes the mountain upon which the Church is built, and on this the foundation hath been digged, and the great stones laid in the trenches with oaths and promises and blood to make them stand secure, even though earth should rock and all creation suffer decay.

APRIL 20.

*T*HERE is none other name under heaven given among men whereby we must be saved, but Jesus Christ and him crucified. There were not two arks, but one ark: so there are not two Saviours, but one Saviour. There was no other means of salvation except the ark: so there is no plan of deliverance except by Jesus Christ, the Saviour of sinners. In vain you climb the lofty top of Sinai. In vain you climb to the highest pinnacles of your self-conceit and your worldly merit: ye shall be drowned —for "other foundation can no man lay than that which is laid—Jesus Christ and him crucified."

APRIL 21.

OH new-born soul, trembling with anxiety, if thou hast not yet beheld the fair face of thy beloved, if thou canst not as yet delight in the majesty of his offices, and the wonders of his person, let thy soul be fully alive to the richness of his grace, and the preciousness of his blood. These thou hast in thy possession, the pledges of thine interest in him; love him then for these, and in due time he will discover unto thee fresh wonders and glories, so that thou shalt be able to exclaim, "O staff of my life and strength of my heart, I will sit and sing under thy shadow, yea, I will sing a song of loves touching MY WELL-BELOVED."

APRIL 22.

IT is the highest stage of manhood to have no wish, no thought, no desire, but Christ—to feel that to die were bliss, if it were for Christ—that to live in penury, and woe, and scorn, and contempt, and misery, were sweet for Christ—to feel that it matters nothing what becomes of one's self, so that our Master is but exalted—to feel that though, like a sere leaf, we are blown in the blast, we are quite careless whither we are going, so long as we feel that the Master's hand is guiding us according to His will.

APRIL 23.

*A*GED and mellow saints have so sweet a savor of Christ in them that their conversation is sweetly refreshing to him who delights to hear of the glories of redeeming love. They have tried the anchor in the hour of storm, they have tested the armor in the day of battle, they have proved the shadow of the great rock in the burning noontide in the weary land; therefore do they talk of those things, and of *Him* who is all these unto them. We must dive into the same waters if we would bring up the same pearls.

APRIL 24.

*A*N honored saint was once so ravished with a revelation of his Lord's love, that feeling his mortal frame to be unable to sustain more of such bliss, he cried, "Hold, Lord, it is enough, it is enough!" In heaven we shall be able to see the bottomless well of love to our lips, and drink on forever. Ah, that will be love indeed which shall overflow our souls forever in our Father's house above! Who can tell the transports, the raptures, the amazements of delight which that love shall beget in us? and who can guess the sweetness of the song, or the swiftness of the obedience which will be the heavenly expressions of love made perfect?

APRIL 25.

*T*HE best enjoyments of Christ on earth are but as the dipping of our finger in water for the cooling of our thirst; but heaven is bathing in seas of bliss: even so our love here is but one drop of the same substance as the waters of the ocean, but not comparable for magnitude or depth. Oh, how sweet it will be to be married to the Lord Jesus, and to enjoy forever, and without any interruption, the heavenly delights of His society! Surely, if a glimpse of Him melteth our soul, the full fruition of Him will be enough to burn up our hearts with affection.

APRIL 26.

*W*HEN the soul is led by the Holy Spirit to take a clear view of Jesus in his various offices, how speedily the heart is on fire with love! To see him stooping from his throne to become man, next yielding to suffering to become man's sympathizing friend, and then bowing to death itself to become his ransom, is enough to stir every passion of the soul. To discern him by faith as the propitiation for sin, sprinkling his own blood within the veil, and nailing our sins to his cross, is a sight which never fails to excite the reverent, yet rapturous admiration of the beholder.

APRIL 27.

CHRIST never lingers long with dumb souls; if there be no crying out to him, he departs. What a marvelous influence prayer has upon our fellowship with Jesus! We may always measure one by the other. Those pray most fervently and frequently who have been constant attendants on the kind Intercessor; while, on the other hand, those who wrestle the hardest in supplication will hold the angel the longest. Joshua's voice stayed the sun in the heavens for a few hours; but the voice of prayer can detain the Sun of righteousness for months and even years.

APRIL 28.

REMEMBER, that in proportion to the fullness of thine heart will be the fullness of thy life. Be empty-hearted and thy life will be a meager skeleton existence. Be full-hearted and thy life will be full and strong, a thing that will tell upon the world. Keep, then, thy peace with God firm within thee. Keep thou close to this, that Jesus Christ hath made peace between thee and God. And keep thy conscience still; then shall thy heart be full and thy soul strong to do thy Master's work. Keep thy peace with God. This will keep thy heart pure.

APRIL 29.

*D*O not be afraid, Christ is your strength and righteousness. A wave comes against the side of the ship, but it does not hurt the ship, it only drives the wedges in tighter. The Master is at the helm—will not that assure your heart? It has floated over so many billows—will not that increase your confidence? It must, indeed, be a strong billow that will sink it now; there never shall be such an one.

Christ presents the perfect number of all his people to the Father in the last day; not one shall perish. The ark of our salvation shall bring all its living freight into the haven of everlasting rest.

APRIL 30.

*T*HIS morning our desires go forth for growth in our acquaintance with the Lord Jesus. This was most blessedly perfect long before we had the slightest knowledge of him. Before we had a being in the world we had a being in his heart. When we were enemies to him, he knew us, our misery and our wickedness. When we wept bitterly in despairing repentance, and viewed him only as a judge and a ruler, he viewed us as his brethren well beloved. He never mistook his chosen, but always beheld them as objects of his infinite affection. "The Lord knoweth them that are his."

MAY 1.

*Y*OU have no place in which to pour your troubles except the ear of God. If you tell them to your friends, you but put your troubles out a moment, and they will return again. Roll your burden unto God, and you have rolled it into a great deep, out of which it will never by any possibility rise. Cast your troubles where you cast your sins; you have cast your sins into the depths of the sea, there cast your troubles also. Never keep a trouble half an hour on your own mind before you tell it to God. As soon as the trouble comes, quick, the first thing, tell it to your Father.

MAY 2.

*I*S my conscience at peace? For, if my heart condemn me not, God is greater than my heart, and doth know all things; if my conscience bear witness with me, that I am a partaker of the precious grace of salvation, then happy am I! I am one of those to whom God hath given the peace which passeth all understanding. Now, why is this called "the peace of God?" Because it comes from God—because it was planned by God—because God gave his Son to make the peace—because God gives his Spirit to give the peace in the conscience—because, indeed, it is God himself in the soul.

MAY 3.

*S*OLDIER of the cross! the hour is coming when the note of victory shall be proclaimed throughout the world. The battlements of the enemy must soon succumb; the swords of the mighty must soon be given up to the Lord of lords. What! soldier of the cross! in the day of victory wouldst thou have it said that thou didst turn thy back in the day of battle? Dost thou not wish to have a share in the conflict, that thou mayest have a share in the victory? If thou hast even the hottest part of the battle, wilt thou falter? Thou shalt have the brightest part of the victory, if thou art in the fiercest of the conflict.

MAY 4.

*I*T is often remarked that after soul sorrow our pastors are more gifted with words in season, and their speech is more full of savor: this is to be accounted for by the sweet influence of grief when sanctified by the Holy Spirit. Blessed Redeemer, we delight in thy love, and thy presence is the light of our joys; but if thy brief withdrawals qualify us for glorifyng thee in cheering thy saints, we thank thee for leaving us; as we seek thee by night, it shall somewhat cheer us that thou art blessing us when thou takest away thy richest blessing.

MAY 5.

*I*T certainly is not possible for us to be in a position where Omnipotence cannot assist us. God hath servants everywhere. There are "treasures hid in the sand," and the Lord's chosen shall eat thereof. When the clouds hide the mountains they are as real as in the sunshine; so the promise and the Providence of God are unchanged by the obscurity of our faith, or the difficulties of our position. There is hope, and hope at hand, therefore, let us be of good cheer.

When we are at our worst let us trust with unshaking faith. Recollect that then is the time when we can most glorify God by faith.

MAY 6.

*T*HE *cross of Christ is Christ's glory.* Man seeks to win his glory by the sacrifice of others —Christ by the sacrifice of himself: men seek to get crowns of gold—he sought a crown of thorns: men think that glory lieth in being exalted over others—Christ thought that his glory did lie in becoming "a worm and no man," a scoff and reproach amongst all that beheld him. He stooped when he conquered; and he counted that the glory lay as much in the stooping as in the conquest.

Our God has made the day spring from on high to visit us. Our life is bright with these visits as the sky with stars.

MAY 7.

STARS may be seen from the bottom of a deep well when they cannot be discerned from the top of a mountain: so are many things learned in adversity which the prosperous man dreams not of. We need affliction as the trees need winter, that we may collect sap and nourishment for future blossoms and fruit. Sorrow is as necessary for the soul as medicine is to the body:

"The path of sorrow, and that path alone,
    Leads to the land where sorrow is unknown."

The adversities of to-day are a preparatory school for the higher learning.

MAY 8.

WHEN heaven smiles and pours down its showers of grace, then they are precious things; but without the celestial rain we might as much expect water from the arid waste, as a real blessing in the use of them. "All my springs are in Thee," is the believer's daily confession to his Lord—a confession which until death must ever be upon his lips. As love comes from heaven, so it must feed on heavenly bread. It cannot exist in the wilderness unless it be fed by manna from on high. Love must feed on love. The very soul and life of our love to God is his love to us.

MAY 9.

*T*HE choicest communications ever made of human minds are those which have come from the Great Father. Say, poor soul, what get you in Christ whenever you go to him? Can you not say, Oh! I get more love to him than I had before; I never approached near to him but I gained a large draught and ample fill of love of God. Out of his fullness we receive grace for grace, and love for love. In a word, by faith we behold the glory of the Lord as in a glass, and are changed into the same image—and the image of God is love. Live upon Christ, who is the daily manna, and you will live well.

MAY 10.

*O*NLY love seeks after love. If I desire the love of another it can surely only be because I myself have love toward him. We care not to be loved by those whom we do not love. It were an embarrassment rather than an advantage to receive love from those to whom we would not return it. When God asks human love, it is because God is love. Whatever our frame or feeling, the heart of Jesus is full of love—love which was not caused by our good behavior, and is not diminished by our follies—love which is as sure in the night of darkness as in the brightness of the day of joy.

MAY 11.

*I*F you would find God, he dwelleth on every hill-top and in every valley; God is everywhere in creation; but if you want a special display of him, if you would know what is the secret place of the tabernacle of the Most High, the inner chamber of divinity, you must go where you find the church of true believers, for it is here he makes his continual residence known—in the hearts of the humble and contrite, who tremble at his word. Every church is to our Lord a more sublime thing than a constellation in the heavens; as he is precious to his saints, so are they precious to him.

MAY 12.

*W*E love Jesus when we are advanced in the divine life, from a participation with him in the great work of his incarnation. We long to see our fellowmen turned from darkness to light, and we love him as the sun of righteousness, who can alone illuminate them. We hate sin, and therefore we rejoice in him as manifested to take away sin. We pant for holier and happier times, and therefore we adore him as the coming Ruler of all lands, who will bring a millennium with him in the day of his appearing. Love the soul of every man with all the intensity of thy being.

MAY 13.

*T*HERE was never a soul yet that sincerely sought the Saviour, who perished before he found him. No; the gates of death shall never shut on thee till the gates of grace have opened for thee; till Christ has washed thy sins away thou shalt never be baptized in Jordan's flood. Thy life is secure, for this is God's constant plan—he keeps his own elect alive till the day of his grace, and then he takes them to himself. And inasmuch as thou knowest thy need of a Saviour, thou art one of his, and thou shalt never die until thou hast found him. God sends the right messenger to the right man.

MAY 14.

*W*E love him because he first loved us." Here is the starting point of love's race. This is the rippling rill which afterwards swells into a river, the torch with which the pile of piety is kindled. The emancipated spirit loves the Saviour for the freedom which he has conferred upon it; it beholds the agony with which the priceless gift was purchased, and it adores the bleeding sufferer for the pains which he so generously endured.

On taking a survey of our whole life, we see that the kindness of God has run all through it like a silver thread.

MAY 15.

*I*F Christ is more excellent at one time than another it certainly is in "the cloudy and dark day." We can never so well see the true color of Christ's love as in the night of weeping. Christ in the dungeon, Christ on the bed of sickness, Christ in poverty, is Christ indeed to a sanctified man. No vision of Christ Jesus is so truly a revelation as that which is seen in the Patmos of suffering. This he proves to his beloved, not by mere words of promise, but by actual deeds of affection. As our sufferings abound, so he makes our consolations to abound.

MAY 16.

*S*UNLIGHT is never more grateful than after a long watch in the midnight blackness; Christ's presence is never more acceptable than after a time of weeping, on account of his departure. It is a sad thing that we should need to lose our mercies to teach us to be grateful for them; let us mourn over this crookedness of our nature; and let us strive to express our thankfulness for mercies, so that we may not have to lament their removal. If thou desirest Christ for a perpetual guest, give him all the keys of thine heart; let not one cabinet be locked up from him; give him the range of every room, and the key of every chamber; thus you will constrain him to remain.

MAY 17.

*W*E never live so well as when we live on the
Lord Jesus simply as he is, and not upon our
enjoyments and raptures. Faith is never more
likely to increase in strength than in times which
seem adverse to her. When she is lightened of
trust in joys, experiences, frames, feelings, and the
like, she rises the nearer heaven. Trust in thy
Redeemer's strength, thou benighted soul; exercise
what faith thou hast, and by and by he shall rise
upon thee with healings beneath his wings. Go
from faith to faith and thou shalt receive blessing
upon blessing.

MAY 18.

*J*UST so far as the Lord shall give us grace to
suffer *for* Christ, to suffer *with* Christ, just
so far does he honor us. Afflictions cannot sanctify
us, except as they are used by Christ, as his mallet
and his chisel. Our joys and our efforts cannot
make us ready for heaven, apart from the hand of
Jesus who fashioneth our hearts aright, and pre-
pareth us to be partakers of the inheritance of the
saints in light. Our griefs cannot mar the melody
of our praise; we reckon them to be the bass part
of our life's song. This vale of tears is but the
pathway to the better country; this world of woe
is but the stepping-stone to a world of bliss.

MAY 19.

CONSIDER the history of the Redeemer's love and a thousand enchanting acts of affection will suggest themselves, all of which have had for their design the weaving of the heart into Christ and the intertwisting of the thoughts and emotions of the renewed soul with the mind of Jesus. Nearness of life towards the Lamb will necessarily involve greatness of love to him. As nearness to the sun increases the temperature of the various planets, so close communion with Jesus raises the heat of the affections towards him. This alone is the true life of a Christian—its source, its sustenance, its fashion, its end, all gathered up in one word—Christ Jesus.

MAY 20.

CHOICE discoveries of the wondrous love and grace of Jesus are most tenderly vouchsafed unto believers in the times of grief. Then it is that he lifts them up from his feet, where, like Mary, it is their delight to sit, and exalts them to the position of the favored John, pressing them to his breast and bidding them lean on his bosom.

The love of Christ in its sweetness, its fullness, its greatness, its faithfulness, passeth all human comprehension.

Heaven on earth is abounding love to Jesus. This is the first and last of true delight—to love him who is the first and the last. To love Jesus is another name for paradise.

MAY 21.

*P*RAYER is the lisping of the believing infant, the shout of the fighting believer, the requiem of the dying saint falling asleep in Jesus. It is the breath, the watchword, the comfort, the strength and honor of a Christian.

Spiritual mercies are good things, and not only good things, but the best things, so that you may well ask for them; for if no good things will be withholden, much more will none of the best things.

If you want power in prayer you must have purity in life.

If our faith is to grow exceedingly we must maintain constant intercourse with God.

MAY 22.

A CHRISTIAN ought to be a comforter, with kind words on his lips and sympathy in his heart; he should carry sunshine wherever he goes, and diffuse happiness around him. If you see Jesus and abide in the light of his countenance habitually, your faces, your characters, your lives will grow resplendent, even without your knowing it. If the tender mercy of God has visited us, and done so much more for us than I can tell or than you can hear, let us ourselves exhibit tender mercy in our dealings with our fellow-men. He lives most and lives best who is the means of imparting spiritual life to others.

MAY 23.

A CLEAR proof of the divine origin of scripture is afforded by its portrait of the Perfect Man. Jesus is sinless in thought, and word, and deed; his enemies are unable to find a fault in him either of excess or defect. Nowhere else in the world have we such another portrait of man; it would be superfluous to say that nowhere have we such another man. Jesus is unique; he is original, with peculiarities all his own, but without any divergence from the straight line of rectitude. He is not a recluse, whose character would have few relationships, and therefore few tests, but one living in the fierce light of a King among men, coming into relation with the world in a thousand ways.

MAY 24.

C ONCERNING the consciousness of evil in the past of our lives and the tendency to wrong-doing in our nature, the Bible is very clear, and it is most admirably explicit as to God's way of removing this barrier to our future progress. In Holy Scripture we see a most wise and gracious method for the putting away of guilt, without injury to the divine justice. The atonement offered by the Lord Jesus, who is the essence of the revelation of God, is an eminently satisfactory solution of the soul's sternest problem. Our feeling is that God, the universal Ruler, must do right, and must not, even for mercy's sake, relax the rule that evil done must bring evil as its consequence.

*M*EADOWS may be occasionally flooded, but the marshes are drowned by the tide at every return thereof."

There is all this difference between the sins of the righteous and those of the ungodly. Surprised by temptation, true saints are flooded with a passing outburst of sin; but the wicked delight in transgression and live in it as in their element. The saint in his errors is a star under a cloud, but the sinner is darkness itself. The gracious may fall into iniquity, but the graceless run into it, wallow in it, and again and again return to it.

MAY 26.

*B*ETWEEN the revelation of God in his word and that in his works, there can be no actual discrepancy. The one may go farther than the other, but the revelation must be harmonious. Between *the interpretation* of the Works and *the interpretation* of the Word, there may be very great differences. It must be admitted that the men of the Book have sometimes missed its meaning. Nay, more: it is certain that, in their desire to defend their Bible, devout persons have been unwise enough to twist its words. If they had always labored to understand what God said, in his book, and had steadfastly adhered to its meaning, they would have been wise.

MAY 27.

*M*OREOVER, we may not refuse reliance upon God on the ground of our insignificance; for it is not conceivable that anything can be too little for God. The wonders of the microscope are quite as remarkable as those of the telescope; we may not set a bound to the Lord in one direction any more than in the other. He can and will show his divine skill in a man's life, as well as in a planet's circuit.

Witnesses are alive to testify to the Lord's making bare his arm on the behalf of them that trust him. Any man may also put the principle to the test in his own instance; and it is memorable that none have done so in vain.

MAY 28.

*I*T has been asserted that God cannot be known. Those who say this declare that they themselves know nothing but phenomena.

He who made the world was certainly an intelligent being, in fact the highest intelligence; for in myriads of ways his works display the presence of profound thought and knowledge. Lord Bacon said, "I had rather believe all the fables of the Talmud and the Koran than that this universal frame is without a mind," This being so, we do in that very fact know God in a measure; ay, and in such a measure that we are prepared to trust him. He that made all things is more truly an object of confidence than all things that he has made.

MAY 29.

SELF-RELIANCE is inculcated as a moral virtue, and in a certain sense, with due surroundings, it is so. Observation and experience show that it is a considerable force in the world. He who questions his own powers, and does not know his own mind, hesitates, trembles, falters, fails; his diffidence is the author of his disappointment. The self-reliant individual hopes, considers, plans, resolves, endeavors, perseveres, succeeds; his assurance of victory is one leading cause of his triumph. A man believes in his own capacity, and unless he is altogether a piece of emptiness he gradually convinces others that his estimate is correct.

MAY 30.

BELOVED reader, what is thy desperate case? What heavy matter hast thou in hand this evening? Bring it hither. The God of the prophets lives, and lives to help his saints. He will not suffer thee to lack any good thing. Believe thou in the Lord of Hosts! Approach him pleading the name of Jesus; thou too shalt see the finger of God working marvels for his people. According to thy faith be it unto thee. In our hours of bodily pain and mental anguish, we find ourselves as naturally driven to prayer as the wreck is driven upon the shore by the waves.

Faith, then, we choose, rather than doubt, as the mainspring of our life.

*P*RAYER must not be our chance work but our daily business, our habit, and vocation. As artists give themselves to their models, and poets to their classical pursuits, so must we addict ourselves to prayer. We must be immersed in prayer as in our element, and so pray without ceasing. Lord, teach us to pray that we may be more prevalent in supplication.

The common fault with the most of us is our readiness to yield to distractions. Our thoughts go roving hither and thither, and we make little progress towards our desired end. Like quicksilver, our mind will not hold together, but rolls off this way and that. How great an evil this is! It injures us, and, what is worse, it insults our God.

JUNE 1.

*O*NE of the marvels of the Bible is its singular fullness. It is not a book of gold leaf beaten thin, as most books are as to thought; but its sentences are nuggets of unalloyed truth. The book of God is clearly the god of books, for it is infinite. Well said a German author, "In this little book is contained all the wisdom of the world."

> "We search the world for truth; we cull
> The good, the pure, the beautiful
> From graven stone and written scroll,
> From all old flower-fields of the soul;
> And, weary seekers of the best,
> We come back laden from the quest,
> To find that all the sages said
> Is in the Book our mothers read."

JUNE 2.

*I*T has been well said, "Nothing is easier than to doubt. A man of moderate ability or learning can doubt more than the wisest men believe." Faith demands knowledge, for it is an intelligent grace, able and anxious to justify itself; but infidelity is not required to give a reason for the doubt that is in it; a defiant mien and a blustering tone answer its purpose. The acme of unbelief is to know nothing. What is this but the apotheosis of ignorance?

A man may glide into agnosticism insensibly, and remain in it languidly; but to believe is to be alive. Those who think faith to be a childish business will have to make considerable advance toward manliness before they are able to test their own theory.

JUNE 3.

*T*HE most important part of human life is not its end, but its beginning. Our death day is the child of the past, but our opening years are the sires of the future. At the last hour men summon to their bedside a solemnity of thought which arrives too late for any practical result. The hush and awe and far-away look, so frequent in departing moments, should have come much sooner. Commend us to the example of the Hebrew king, who fasted and wore sackcloth while the child was yet alive. Wisely did he foresee the uselessness of lamenting when the scene should close. "Can I bring him back again?" is one of the most serious of questions.

JUNE 4.

*L*ADEN boughs hang low. The nettle mounteth above its fellow weeds, but the violet lieth shrouded under its leaves, and is only found out by its own scent." Walking one day by a stream we were conscious of a delicious perfume, and only then did we perceive the little blue eyes which were look-ing up to us so meekly from the ground on which we stood. Virtue is always modest, and modesty is itself a virtue. He who is discovered by his real excellence, and not by his egotistical advertisements of his own perfections, is a man worth knowing.

JUNE 5.

YOU may have sunk low in despondency, and even despair; but if your soul has any longing towards Christ, and if you are seeking to rest in his finished work, God sees the "light." He not only *sees* it, but he also *preserves* it in you. "I, the Lord, do keep it." Sometimes *we* cannot see the light, but *God* always sees the light, and that is much better than our seeing it. If the Lord has given you light, dear reader, he looks on that light with peculiar interest; for not only is it dear to him as his own handiwork, but because it is *like* himself, for "he is light."

JUNE 6.

MANY can bring the Scriptures to the mind, but the Lord alone can prepare the mind to receive the Scriptures. Our Lord Jesus differs from all other teachers; they reach the ear, but he instructs the heart; they deal with the outward letter, but he imparts an inward taste for the truth, by which we perceive its savor and spirit. The most unlearned of men become ripe scholars in the school of grace when the Lord Jesus by his Holy Spirit unfolds the mysteries of the kingdom to them, and grants the divine anointing by which they are enabled to behold the invisible. Happy are we if we have had our understandings cleared and strengthened by the Master!

JUNE 7.

*W*E are never out of the reach of temptation. Both at home and abroad, we are liable to meet with allurements to evil; the morning opens with peril, and the shades of evening find us still in jeopardy. They are well kept whom God keeps, but woe unto those who go forth into the world, or even dare to walk their own house unarmed. Those who think themselves secure, are more exposed to danger than any others. The armor-bearer of Sin is Self-confidence. Be not secure. We need a watchman for the night, as well as a guardian for the day. Oh, for the constraining love of Jesus to keep us active and useful!

JUNE 8.

*W*HEN the beams of the sun are contracted by a burning-glass, upon one spot, then they cause fire, so when our thoughts are concentrated on one object they warm the heart and at last burn the truth into it."

There are many rays of light, but they are scattered. We get a little upon many things, while what is wanted is one great truth, and so much upon it as shall fix it on the heart, and set the soul blazing with it. This is the fault of many lives: they are squandered upon a dozen objects, whereas if they were economized for one, they would be mighty lives, known in the present and honored in the future.

JUNE 9.

*T*HE unsoundness of a vessel is not seen when it is empty; but when it is filled with water, then we shall see whether it will leak or no."

It is in our prosperity that we are tested. Men are not fully discovered to themselves till they are tried by fullness of success. Praise finds pride, wealth reveals selfishness, and learning discovers the leak of unbelief. Success is the crucible of character. Hence the prosperity which some welcome as an unmixed favor may far more rightly be regarded as an intense form of test. O Lord, preserve us when we are full as much as when we are empty.

JUNE 10.

A GARRISON is not free from danger while it hath an enemy lodged within."

You may bolt all your doors, and fasten all your windows, but if the thieves have placed even a little child within doors, who can draw the bolts for them, the house is still unprotected. All the sea outside a ship cannot do it damage till the water enters within and fills the hold. Hence, it is clear, our greatest danger is from within. All the devils in hell and tempters on earth could do us no injury if there were no corruption in our nature. Alas, our heart is our greatest enemy; this is the little home-born thief.

JUNE 11.

WE are not exacting when we demand that each candid man should read the Bible for himself. In testing a book, which professes to be the revelation of God's mind, we shall act unworthily if we trust to others, be they who they may. Second-hand information lacks assurance and vividness; a personal investigation is far more satisfactory and beneficial. Many other books have been warmly praised by their readers; but we have never yet met with any other volume which has commanded such frequent enthusiasm and such devoted affection as the Bible: neither have we heard of one which answers so many and such divers purposes in connection with the lives of men.

JUNE 12.

CHRIST had no transgressions of his own; he took ours upon his head; he never committed a wrong, but he took all my sin, and all yours, if ye are believers; concerning all his people, it is true, he bore their griefs and carried their sorrows in his own body on the tree. Sin may drag thee ever so low, but Christ's great atonement is still under all. You may have descended into the deeps, but you cannot have fallen so low as "the uttermost;" and to the uttermost he saves.

To-day *the world's one and only remedy* is the cross.

JUNE 13.

*B*UT we do not observe God's hand as much as we should. Our good puritanic forefathers, when it rained, used to say, that God had unstopped the bottles of heaven. When it rains nowadays, we think the clouds have become condensed. If they had a field of hay cut, they used to plead of the Lord that he would bid the sun shine. We, perhaps, are wiser, as we think; and we consider it hardly worth while to pray about such things, thinking they will come in the course of nature. They believed that God was in every storm; nay, in every cloud of dust. They used to speak of a present God in everything.

JUNE 14.

*B*UT how is this to be? How is the world to be brought back? How is it to be restored? We answer, the reason why there was this original harmony between earth and heaven was because there was love between them twain, and our great reason for hoping that there shall be at last re-established an undiscordant harmony between heaven and earth is simply this, that God hath already manifested his love toward us, and that in return, hearts touched by his grace do even now love him; and when they shall be multiplied, and love re-established, then shall harmony be complete.

*L*OSSES, too, are frequently the means God uses to fetch home his wandering sheep; like fierce dogs, they bring wanderers back to the shepherd. How often have we seen the Christian rendered obedient to his Lord's will by straightness of bread and hard labor. When rich and increased with goods, many professors carry their heads much too loftily, and speak much too boastfully. Like David, they boast: "My mountain standeth fast; it shall never be moved." When the Christian groweth wealthy, is in good repute, hath good health, and a happy family, he too often wanders away. If he be a true child of God, there is a rod preparing for him.

JUNE 16.

*F*RIENDSHIP is the only thing in the world concerning the usefulness of which all mankind are agreed. Friendship seems as necessary an element of a comfortable existence in this world as fire and water, or even air itself. A man may drag along a miserable existence in proud solitary dignity, but his life is scarce life; it is nothing but an existence, the tree of life being stripped of the leaves of hope and the fruits of joy. He who would be happy here must have friends; and he who would be happy hereafter, must, above all things, find a friend in the world to come in the person of God, the Father of his people.

JUNE 17.

SOMETIMES Saul was among the prophets, easily turned into a prophet, and then afterwards among the witches; sometimes in one place and then another, and insincere in everything. How many such we have in every Christian assembly; men who are very easily molded. They have affectionate dispositions, very likely a tender conscience; but then the conscience is so remarkably tender, that when touched it seems to give, and you are afraid to probe deeper; it heals as soon as it is wounded. You may press them whichever way you wish, they are so elastic you can always effect your purpose, but then they are not fixed in character and soon return to be what they were before.

JUNE 18.

ABIDE with us, for the day is far spent." Beloved, remember what you have heard of your Lord Jesus, and what he has done for you; make your heart the golden pot of manna to preserve the memorial of the heavenly bread whereon you have fed in days gone by. Let your memory treasure up everything about Christ which you have either felt, or known, or believed, and then let your fond affections hold *him* fast forevermore. Love the person of your Lord! Bring forth the alabaster box of your heart, even though it be broken, and let all the precious ointment of your affection come streaming on his pierced feet.

JUNE 19.

*P*RAY God to send a few men with what the Americans call "grit" in them; men, who when they know a thing to be right, will not turn away, or turn aside, or stop; men who will persevere all the more because there are difficulties to meet or foes to encounter; who stand all the more true to their Master because they are opposed; who, the more they are thrust into the fire, the hotter they become, who, just like the bow, the further the string is drawn the more powerfully it sends forth its arrows, and so the more they are trodden upon, the more mighty will they become in the cause of truth against error.

JUNE 20.

*R*ETURN unto thy rest, O my soul, for the Lord hath dealt bountifully with thee." It was at the still hour, when the gates of the day were closing, that with weary wing the dove came back to her master: O Lord, enable me this evening thus to return to Jesus. She could not endure to spend a night hovering over the restless waste, nor can I bear to be even for another hour away from Jesus, the rest of my heart, the home of my spirit. She did not merely alight upon the roof of the ark, she "came into him;" even so would my longing spirit look into the secret of the Lord, pierce to the interior of truth, enter into that which is within the veil, and reach to my Beloved in very deed.

*F*AITHFULNESS to us in our faults is a certain sign of fidelity in a friend. You may depend upon that man who will tell you of your faults in a kind and considerate manner. Give me for a friend a man who will speak honestly of me before my face; who will not tell first one neighbor, and then another, but who will come straight to my house and say: "I feel there is a wrong in you, my brother, I must tell you of." That man is a true friend; he has proved himself to be so; for we never get any praise for telling people of their faults; we rather hazard their dislike; a man will sometimes thank you for it; but he does not often like you any the better.

JUNE 22.

*W*HAT we are taught to seek or shun in prayer, we should equally pursue or avoid in action. Very earnestly, therefore, should we avoid temptation, seeking to walk guardedly in the path of obedience. We are not to enter the thicket in search of the lion. This lion may cross our path, or leap upon us from the thicket; but we have nothing to do with hunting him. He that meeteth with him, even though he winneth the day, will find it a stern struggle. Let the Christian pray that he may be spared the encounter. Our Saviour, who had experience of what temptation meant, thus earnestly admonished his disciples: "Pray that ye enter not into temptation."

JUNE 23.

YOU know in a wheel there is one portion that never turns round, that stands steadfast, and that is the axle. So, in God's Providence there is an axle which never moves. Christian, here is a sweet thought for thee! Thy state is ever changing: sometimes thou art exalted, and sometimes depressed; yet there is an unmoving point in thy state. What is that axle? What is the pivot upon which all the machinery revolves? It is the axle of God's everlasting love towards his covenant people. The exterior of the wheel is changing; but the center stands forever fixed. Other things may move; but God's love never moves; it is the axle of the wheel, and will endure.

JUNE 24.

FIRST, then, HERE IS WHAT THEY ARE TO TELL. It is to be a story of *personal experience.* "Go home to thy friends and tell them how great things the Lord has done for thee, and hath had compassion on thee." Not what you have believed, but what you have *felt;* what you really know to be your own; not what great things you have read, but what great things the Lord hath *done for you;* not alone what you have seen done in the great congregation, and how great sinners have turned to God, but what the Lord has done for *you.* And mark this: There is never a more interesting story than that which a man tells about himself.

JUNE 25.

*E*VER to be remembered is that best and brightest of hours when first we saw the Lord, lost our burden, received the roll of promise, rejoiced in full salvation, and went on our way in peace. It was spring time in the soul; the winter was past. Then the flowers appeared in our heart: hope, love, peace and patience sprung from the sod; and our resolve was, "Lord, I am thine, wholly thine; all I am, and all I have, I would devote to thee. Thou hast bought me with thy blood; let me spend myself and be spent in thy service. In life and in death let me be consecrated to thee." *How have we kept this resolve?*

JUNE 26.

When thou shalt make his soul an offering for sin, he shall see his seed.—Isa. liii. 10.

*O*UR Lord Jesus has not died in vain. His death was sacrificial; he died as our substitute, because death was the penalty of our sins, and because his substitution was accepted of God. He has saved those for whom he made his soul a sacrifice. By death he became like the corn of wheat, which bringeth forth much fruit.—There must be a succession of children to Jesus; he is "the Father of the everlasting age." He shall say, "Behold, I and the children whom thou hast given me."

JUNE 27.

*M*Y own sight of the precious blood is for my comfort; but it is the Lord's sight of it which secures my safety. Even when I am unable to behold it, the Lord looks at it, and passes over me because of it. None can tell His delight in Jesus. Now rest we in calm security. We have God's sacrifice and God's word to create in us a sense of perfect security. He will, He must, pass over us, because He spared not our glorious substitute. Justice joins hands with love to provide everlasting salvation for all the blood-besprinkled ones.

JUNE 28.

*T*HE branch is not only ever near the stem, but ever receiving life and fruitfulness from it. All true believers abide in Christ in a sense; but there is a higher meaning and this we must know before we gain unlimited power at the throne. "Ask what ye will" is for Enochs who walk with God, for Johns who lie in the Lord's bosom, for those whose union with Christ leads to constant communion.

If you would be mighty in your pleadings, the Lord himself must abide in you, and you in Him.

JUNE 29.

Be careful for nothing; but in everything by prayer and supplication with thanksgiving let your requests be made known unto God. And the peace of God which passeth all understanding, shall keep your hearts and minds through Christ Jesus.—Phil. iv. 6, 7.

NO care but all prayer. No anxiety, but much joyful communion with God. Carry your desires to the Lord of your life, the guardian of your soul. Go to Him with two portions of prayer, and one of fragrant praise. Do not pray doubtfully, but thankfully. Consider that you have your petitions, and, therefore, thank God for His Grace.

JUNE 30.

When a man's ways please the Lord, He maketh even his enemies to be at peace with him.—Prov. xvi. 7.

I MUST see that my ways please the Lord. Even then I shall have enemies; and, perhaps all the more certainly because I endeavored to do that which is right. But what a promise this is! The Lord will make the wrath of men to praise Him, and abate it so that it shall not distress me. When I meet death, who is called the last enemy, I pray that I may be at peace. Only let my great care be to please the Lord in all things.

JULY 1.

ETURN unto the Lord thy God.' Where we first found salvation we shall find it again. At the foot of Christ's cross, confessing sin. Moreover, the Lord will have us obey His voice according to all that He has commanded us, and we must do this with all our heart and all our soul, and then our captivity shall end.

Often depression of spirit and great misery of soul are removed as soon as we quit our idols and bow ourselves to obedience before the living God. We may return to Zion's citizenship, and that speedily. Lord, turn our captivity!

JULY 2.

RIENDSHIP, however, though very pleasing and exceedingly blessed, has been the cause of the greatest misery to men when it has been unworthy and unfaithful; for just in proportion as a good friend is sweet, a false friend is full of bitterness. "A faithless friend is sharper than an adder's tooth." It is sweet to repose in some one; but O! how bitter to have that support snapped, and to receive a grievous fall as the effect of your confidence. Solomon declares that "there is a friend that sticketh closer than a brother." That friend, I suppose, he never found in the pomps and vanities of the world. He had tried them all, but he found them empty; he passed through all their joys.

JULY 3.

*C*OULD faith believe in a Being more answerable to all our needs, more helpful to our noblest longings? Allied to Jesus, we confidently aspire to such likeness to our Creator as it is possible for a creature to bear. Nor is the advantage less in the other direction, for here is a Man, bound to us by relationship and affection the most intense, who is not only tender to the last degree of our suffering nature, but is also as wise as he is brotherly, and as mighty to subdue our faults as he is gentle to bear with our frailties. His Manhood brings Jesus down to us, but united with the divine nature it lifts us up to God. The Lord Jesus thus not only ministers to our comfort, but to our betterment, the greater concern.

JULY 4.

*A*LL they that heard it wondered at those things." We must not cease to wonder at the great marvels of our God. It would be very difficult to draw a line between holy wonder and *real worship;* for when the soul is overwhelmed with the majesty of God's glory, though it may not express itself in song, or even utter its voice with bowed head and humble prayer, yet it silently adores. Our incarnate God is to be worshiped as "the Wonderful." That God should consider his fallen creature, man, and should himself undertake to be man's Redeemer, and to pay his ransom price, is, indeed, marvelous!

JULY 5.

CHRIST will be master of the heart, and sin must be mortified. If your *life* is unholy your *heart* is unchanged; you are an unsaved person. If the Saviour has not sanctified you, renewed you, given you a hatred of sin and a love of holiness, the grace which does not make a man better than others is a worthless counterfeit. Christ saves his people, not *in* their sins, but *from* them. "Without holiness no man shall see the Lord." "Let every one that nameth the name of Christ depart from iniquity." If not saved from sin, how shall we hope to be counted among his people. Lord, save me even now from all evil, and enable me to honor my Saviour.

JULY 6.

HE purgeth it, that it may bring forth more fruit." If you bring forth fruit, you will have to endure affliction. But this affliction works out such precious results, that the Christian who is the subject of it must learn to rejoice in tribulations, because as his tribulations abound, so his consolations abound by Christ Jesus. Rest assured, if you are a child of God, you will be no stranger to the rod. Sooner or later every bar of gold must pass through the fire. You will be delivered from clinging to the present, and made to long for those eternal things which are so soon to be revealed to you.

JULY 7.

GOD ordains with accurate wisdom the most fitting time for the redeemed to abide below. Surely, if there could be regrets in heaven, the saints might mourn that they did not live longer here to do more good. Oh, for more sheaves for my Lord's garner! more jewels for his crown! But how, unless there be more work? When we are fully serving God, and he is giving us to scatter precious seed, and reap a hundredfold, we would even say it is well for us to abide where we are. Whether our Master shall say "go," or "stay," let us be equally well pleased, so long as he indulges us with his presence.

JULY 8.

AS an encouragement cheerfully to offer intercessory prayer, remember that *such prayer is the sweetest God ever hears,* for the prayer of Christ is of this character. His intercession must be the most acceptable of all supplications—and the more like our prayer is to Christ's, the sweeter it will be; thus while petitions for ourselves will be accepted, our pleadings for others, having in them more of the fruits of the Spirit, more love, more faith, more brotherly kindness, will be, through the precious merits of Jesus, the sweetest oblation that we can offer to God, the very fat of our sacrifice. Remember, again, that *intercessory prayer is exceedingly prevalent.* What wonders it has wrought!

JULY 9.

*I*T is true I am weak in faith, and prone to fall, but my very feebleness is the reason why I should always be where thou feedest thy flock, that I may be strengthened and preserved in safety beside the still waters. Why should I turn aside? There is no reason why I should, but there are a thousand reasons why I should not, for Jesus beckons me to come. If he withdraw himself a little, it is but to make me prize his presence more. Now that I am grieved and distressed at being away from him, he will lead me yet again to that sheltered nook where the lambs of his fold are sheltered from the burning sun.

JULY 10.

*W*ITHOUT him we can do nothing, but by his almighty energy the most extraordinary results can be produced: everything depends upon his manifesting or concealing his power. Do we always look up to him both for our inner life and our outward service with the respectful dependence which is fitting? Do we not too often run before his call and act independently of his aid? Let us humble ourselves this day for past neglects, and now entreat the heavenly dew to rest upon us, the sacred oil to anoint us, the celestial flame to burn within us. The Holy Ghost is no temporary gift, he abides with the saints. We have but to seek him aright, and he will be found of us.

JULY 11.

*T*HE *sovereign choice* of the Father, by which he elected us unto eternal life, or ever the earth was, is a matter of vast antiquity, since no date can be conceived for it by the mind of man. We were chosen from before the foundations of the world. *Everlasting love* went with the choice, for it was not a bare act of divine will by which we were set apart, but the divine affections were concerned. The Father loved us in and from the beginning. Here is a theme for daily contemplation. *The eternal purpose* to redeem us from our foreseen ruin, to cleanse and sanctify us, and at last to glorify us, was of infinite antiquity, and runs side by side with immutable love and absolute sovereignty.

JULY 12.

*W*E have not so clear a view of him as we could wish; we know not the heights and depths of his love; but we know of a surety that he is too good to withdraw from a trembling soul the gift which it has been able to obtain. If we have faith as a grain of mustard seed, salvation is our present and eternal possession. If we cannot clasp the Lord in our hands with Simeon, if we dare not lean our heads upon his bosom with John, yet if we can venture in the press behind him, and touch the hem of his garment, we are made whole. Courage, timid one! thy faith hath saved thee; go in peace. *"Being justified by faith, we have peace with God."*

JULY 13.

"WHEREBY they have made thee glad." And who are thus privileged to make the Saviour glad? His Church—his people. But is it possible? He makes *us* glad, but how can *we make him glad?* By *our love*. See, loving heart, how he delights in you. When you lean your head on his bosom, you not only receive, but you give him joy; when you gaze with love upon his all-glorious face, you not only obtain comfort, but impart delight. Our *praise*, too, gives him joy—not the song of the lips alone, but the melody of the heart's deep gratitude. He loves us, not for the value of what we give, but for the motive from which the gift springs.

JULY 14.

IF the Lord be with us through life, we need not fear for our dying confidence; for *when we come to die,* we shall find that "the Lord is *there;"* where the billows are most tempestuous, and the water is most chill, we shall feel the bottom, and know that it is good: our feet shall stand upon the Rock of Ages when time is passing away. Beloved, from the first of a Christian's life to the last, the only reason why he does not perish is because *"the Lord is there."* When the God of everlasting love shall change and leave his elect to perish, then may the Church of God be destroyed; but not till then, because it is written, JEHOVAH SHAMMAH, *"the Lord is there."*

JULY 15.

COMMON, too common is the sin of forgetting the Holy Spirit. This is folly and ingratitude. He deserves well at our hands, for He is good, supremely good. As God, He is *good essentially.* He shares in the threefold ascription of Holy, holy, holy, which ascends to the Triune Jehovah. Unmixed purity, and truth, and grace is He. He is *good benevolently,* tenderly bearing with our waywardness, striving with our rebellious wills; quickening us from our death in sin, and then training us for the skies as a loving nurse fosters her child. How generous, forgiving, and tender is this patient Spirit of God.

JULY 16.

HE first findeth his own brother Simon." Let thy religion begin at home, have a care to put forth the sweetest fruit of spiritual life and testimony in thine own family. You may be very deficient in talent yourself, and yet you may be the means of drawing to Christ one who shall become eminent in grace and service. Ah! dear friend, you little know the possibilities which are in you. You may but speak a word to a child, and in that child there may be slumbering a noble heart which shall stir the Christian church in years to come. Andrew has only two talents, but he finds Peter. Go thou and do likewise.

JULY 17.

IT is quite certain that those whom Christ has washed in His precious blood need not make a confession of sin, as culprits or criminals, before God the Judge, for Christ has forever taken away all their sins, so that they no longer stand where they can be condemned; but having become children, and offending as children, ought they not every day to go before their heavenly Father and confess their sin, and acknowledge their iniquity? Nature teaches that it is the duty of erring children to make a confession to their earthly father, and the grace of God in the heart teaches us that we, as Christians, owe the same duty to our heavenly Father.

JULY 18.

WE should be abler teachers of others, and less liable to be carried about by every wind of doctrine, if we sought to have a more intelligent understanding of the Word of God. As the Holy Ghost, the Author of the Scriptures, is He who alone can enlighten us rightly to understand them, we should constantly ask His teaching, and His guidance into all truth.

Therefore if, for your own and others' profiting, you desire to be "filled with the knowledge of God's will in all wisdom and spiritual understanding," remember that prayer is your best means of study. You may force your way through anything with the leverage of prayer.

JULY 19.

"THE Lord is slow to anger, and great in power," but the greatness of His power brings us mercy. Dear reader, what is your state this day? Can you by humble faith look to Jesus and say, "My substitute, Thou art my rock, my trust"? Then, beloved, be not afraid of God's power; for now that you are forgiven and accepted, now that by faith you have fled to Christ for refuge, the power of God need no more terrify you, than the shield and sword of the warrior need terrify those whom he loves. Rather rejoice that He who is "great in power" is your Father and Friend.

JULY 20.

YOU have not the making of your own cross, your cross is prepared and appointed for you by divine love, and you are cheerfully to accept it. This day Jesus bids you submit your shoulder to His easy yoke. Jesus was a cross-bearer; He leads the way in the path of sorrow. Surely you could not desire a better guide! And if He carries a cross, what nobler burden would you desire? The *Via Crucis* is the way of safety; fear not to tread its thorny paths.

It is a wooden cross, and a man can carry it, for the Man of Sorrows tried the load. Take up your cross, and by the power of the Spirit of God you will soon love it.

JULY 21.

*T*HERE are occasions when God's servants shrink from duty. But what is the consequence? *They lose the presence and comfortable enjoyment of God's love.* When *we* obey our Lord Jesus as believers should, our God is with us; and though we have the whole world against us, if we have God with us, what does it matter? But the moment we start back, and seek our own inventions, we are at sea without a pilot. Then may we bitterly lament and groan out, "O my God, where hast thou gone? How could I have been so foolish as to lose all the bright shinings of thy face? This is a price too high. Let me return to my allegiance, that I may rejoice in thy presence."

JULY 22.

*W*HEN God seems most to leave his church, his heart is warm towards her. History shows us that whenever God uses a rod to chasten his servants, he always breaks it afterwards, as if he loathed the rod which gave his children pain. "Like as a father pitieth his children, so the Lord pitieth them that fear him." His blows are no evidences of want of love. You may fear that the Lord has passed you by, but it is not so: he who counts the stars, and calls them by their names, is in no danger of forgetting his own children. He knows your case as thoroughly as if you were the only creature he ever made, or the only saint he ever loved. Approach him and be at peace.

*T*HOSE goings forth have been from of old, from everlasting." The Lord Jesus had goings forth for his people, *as their representative before the throne, long before they appeared upon the stage of time.* It was "from everlasting" that he signed the compact with his Father, that he would pay blood for blood, suffering for suffering, agony for agony, and death for death, in the behalf of his people; it was "from everlasting" that he gave himself up, without a murmuring word. His goings forth as our Surety were from everlasting. Pause, my soul, and wonder! Thou hadst goings forth in the person of Jesus "from everlasting."

*N*OT only when thou wast born into the world did Christ love thee, but his delights were with the sons of men before there were any sons of men. Often did he think of them; from everlasting to everlasting he had set his affections upon them. I am sure he would not have loved me so long if he had not been a changeless Lover. If he could grow weary of me he would have been tired of me long before now. If he had not loved me with a love as deep as life and as strong as death, he would have turned from me long ago. Oh, joy above all joys, to know that I am his everlasting and inalienable inheritance, given to him by his Father.

*M*IGHT not Jesus well say to us, "I have somewhat against thee, because thou hast left thy first love?" Alas! it is but little we have done for our Master's glory. Our winter has lasted all too long. We give to God pence when he deserveth pounds, nay, deserveth our heart's blood to be coined in the service of his church and of his truth. But shall we continue this? O Lord, after thou hast so richly blessed us, shall we be ungrateful, and become indifferent to thy good cause and work? O quicken us that we may return to our first love, and do our first works! Send us a genial spring, O Sun of Righteousness.

JULY 26.

*B*LESSED Lord Jesus, be with me, reveal thyself, and abide with me all night, so that when I awake, I may be still with thee. I note that the dove brought in her mouth an olive branch plucked off, the memorial of the past day, and a prophecy of the future. Have I no pleasing record to bring home? No pledge and earnest of loving-kindness yet to come? Yes, my Lord, I present thee my grateful acknowledgements for tender mercies which have been new every morning and fresh every evening; and now, I pray thee, put forth thy hand and take thy dove into thy bosom.

JULY 27.

*A*S the Spirit of God descended upon the Lord Jesus, the head, so he also, in measure, descends upon the members of the mystical body. His descent is to us after the same fashion as that in which it fell upon our Lord. There is often a singular *rapidity* about it; or ever we are aware, we are impelled onward and heavenward beyond all expectation. The brooding of the Spirit of God upon the face of the deep, first produced *order and life,* and in our hearts he causes and fosters new life and light. Blessed Spirit, as thou didst rest upon our dear Redeemer, even so rest thou upon us from this time forward and forever.

JULY 28.

The barrel of meal wasted not, neither did the cruse of oil fail, according to the word of the Lord, which He spake by Elijah.

*Y*OU, dear reader, have daily necessities, and because they come so frequently, you are apt to fear that the barrel of meal will one day be empty, and the cruse of oil will fail you. Rest assured that, according to the Word of God, this shall not be the case. Each day, though it bring its trouble, shall bring its help; and though you should live to outnumber the years of Methuselah, and though your needs should be as many as the sands of the seashore, yet shall God's grace and mercy last through all your necessities, and you shall never know a real lack.

*W*ORDS cannot set forth the preciousness of the Lord Jesus to his people. Dear reader, what wouldst thou do in the world without him, in the midst of its temptations and its cares? What wouldst thou do in the morning without him, when thou wakest up and lookest forward to the day's battle? What wouldst thou do at night, when thou comest home jaded and weary, if there were no door of fellowship between thee and Christ? Blessed be his name, he will not suffer us to try our lot without him, for Jesus never forsakes his own. Yet, let the thought of *what life would be without him.* enhance his preciousness.

JULY 30.

*B*E not content with an interview now and then, but seek always to retain his company, for only in his presence hast thou either comfort or safety. Jesus should not be unto us a friend who calls upon us now and then, but one with whom we walk evermore. Thou hast a difficult road before thee; see, O traveler to heaven, that thou go not without thy guide. Thou hast to pass through the fiery furnace; enter it not, unless, like Shadrach, Meshach, and Abednego, thou hast the Son of God to be thy companion. In every condition thou wilt need Jesus. Keep close to thy Best Friend, and he will refresh and cheer thee

*T*HERE is a time appointed for weakness and sickness, when we shall have to glorify God by suffering, and not by earnest activity. There is no single point in which we can hope to escape from the sharp arrows of affliction; out of our few days there is not one secure from sorrow. Beloved reader, set not your affections upon things of earth; but seek those things which are above, for *here* the moth devoureth, and the thief breaketh through, but *there* all joys are perpetual and eternal. The path of trouble is the way home. Lord, make this thought a pillow for many a weary head!

AUGUST 1.

COMMUNION with Christ is a certain cur for every ill. Whether it be the wormwood of woe, or the cloying surfeit of earthly delight, close fellowship with the Lord Jesus will take bitterness from the one, and satiety from the other. Live near to Jesus, Christian, and it is matter of secondary importance whether thou livest on the mountain of honor or in the valley of humiliation. Living near to Jesus, thou art covered with the wings of God, and underneath thee are the everlasting arms. Let nothing keep thee from that hallowed intercourse, which is the choice privilege of a soul wedded to THE WELL-BELOVED.

AUGUST 2.

DOUBTLESS the reader has been tried with the temptation to rely upon things which are seen, instead of resting alone upon the invisible God. Christians often look to man for help and counsel, and mar the noble simplicity of their reliance upon their God. Does this portion meet the eye of a child of God anxious about temporals, then would we reason with him a while. You trust in Jesus, and only in Jesus, for your salvation; then why are you troubled? *"Because of my great care."* Is it not written, "Cast thy burden upon the Lord?" "Be careful for nothing, but in everything by prayer and supplication make known your wants unto God."

AUGUST 3.

*T*HOUGH the host that feeds at Jehovah's table is countless as the stars of heaven, yet each one has his portion of meat. Think how much grace one saint requires; so much that nothing but the Infinite could supply him for one day; and yet the Lord spreads his table, not for one, but many saints; not for one day, but for many years. The guests at mercy's banquet are satisfied, nay, more "abundantly satisfied;" and that not with ordinary fare, but with fatness, the peculiar fatness of God's own house; and such feasting is guaranteed by a faithful promise to all those children of men who put their trust under the shadow of Jehovah's wings.

AUGUST 4.

*T*HIS is no unusual occurrence; it is the general rule of the moral universe that those men prosper who do their work with all their hearts, while those are almost certain to fail who go to their labor leaving half their hearts behind them. God does not give harvests to idle men, except harvests of thistles, nor is he pleased to send wealth to those who will not dig in the field to find its hid treasure. It is universally confessed that if man would prosper, he must be diligent in business. It is the same in religion as it is in other things. If you would prosper in your work for Jesus, let it be *heart* work, and let it be done with *all* your heart.

AUGUST 5.

*H*OW constantly our Master used the title, the "Son of Man!" If he had chosen, he might always have spoken of himself as the Son of God, the Everlasting Father, the Wonderful, the Counselor, the Prince of Peace; but behold the lowliness of Jesus! He prefers to call himself the Son of man. Let us learn a lesson of humility from our Saviour. Jesus loved manhood so much, that he delighted to honor it; and since it is a high honor, and, indeed, the greatest dignity of manhood, that Jesus is the Son of man, he is wont to display this name, that he may, as it were, hang royal stars upon the breast of manhood, and show forth the love of God to Abraham's seed.

AUGUST 6.

*W*HENEVER we are privileged to eat of the bread which Jesus gives, we are satisfied with the full and sweet repast. When Jesus is the host, no guest goes empty from the table. Our *head* is satisfied with the precious truth which Christ reveals; our *heart* is content with Jesus, our *hope* is satisfied, for whom have we in heaven but Jesus? and our *desire* is satiated, for what can we wish for more than "to know Christ and to be found in him?" Jesus fills our *conscience,* till it is at perfect peace; our judgment with the certainty of his teachings; our *memory* with recollections of what he has done, and our *imagination* with the prospects of what he is yet to do.

AUGUST 7.

"Canst thou bind the sweet influences of Pleiades, or loose the bands of Orion?"

HE looses the bands of Orion, and none but he. What a blessing it is that he can do it! O that he would perform the wonder to-night! Lord, end my winter, and let my spring begin. I cannot, with all my longings, raise my soul out of her death and dullness, but all things are possible with thee. I need celestial influences, the clear shinings of thy love, the beams of thy grace, the light of thy countenance; these are the Pleiades to me. I suffer much from sin and temptation; these are my wintry signs, my terrible Orion. Lord, work wonders in me, and for me. Amen.

AUGUST 8.

THE Saviour was "a man of sorrows," but every thoughtful mind has discovered the fact that down deep in His innermost soul He carried an inexhaustible treasury of refined and heavenly joy. Of all the human race, there was never a man who had a deeper, purer, or more abiding peace than our Lord Jesus Christ. "He was anointed with the oil of gladness above His fellows." His vast benevolence must have afforded Him the deepest possible delight, for benevolence is joy. There were a few remarkable seasons when this joy manifested itself. "At that hour Jesus rejoiced in spirit, and said, I thank Thee, O Father, Lord of heaven and earth."

AUGUST 9.

*H*OLD thou me up, and I shall be safe."
Having prayed, you must also watch; guarding every thought, word, and action with holy jealousy. Do not expose yourself unnecessarily; but if called to exposure, if you are bidden to go where the darts are flying, never venture forth without your shield; for the devil will rejoice that his hour of triumph is come, and will soon make you fall down wounded by his arrows. Though slain you cannot be, wounded you may be. "Be sober, be vigilant; danger may be in an hour when all seemeth securest to thee." Therefore take heed to thy ways, and watch unto prayer. May the Holy Spirit guide us in all our ways.

AUGUST 10.

*S*ON OF MAN—whenever He said that word, He shed a halo round the head of Adam's children. Jesus Christ called Himself the Son of man to express His oneness and sympathy with His people. He thus reminds us that He is one whom we may approach without fear. As a man, we may take to Him all our griefs and troubles, for He knows them by experience; in that He Himself hath suffered as the "Son of man," He is able to succor and comfort us. All hail, Thou blessed Jesus! inasmuch as Thou art evermore using the sweet name which acknowledges that Thou art a brother and a near kinsman, it is to us a dear token of Thy grace, Thy humility, Thy love.

AUGUST 11.

*W*HOLE-HEARTEDNESS shows itself in *perseverance;* there may be failure at first, but the earnest worker will say, "It is the Lord's work, and it must be done; my Lord has bidden me do it, and in His strength I will accomplish it." Christian, art thou thus "with all thine heart" serving thy Master? Remember the earnestness of Jesus! Think what heart-work was His! He could say, *"The zeal of Thine house hath eaten Me up."* When He sweat great drops of blood, it was no light burden he had to carry upon those blessed shoulders; and when He poured out His heart, it was no weak effort He was making for the salvation of His people.

AUGUST 12.

*W*HETHER we speak of the active or passive righteousness of Christ there is an equal fragrance. There was a sweet savor in His active life by which He honored the law of God, and made every precept to glitter like a precious jewel in the pure setting of His own person. Such, too, was His passive obedience, when He endured, with un-murmuring submission, hunger and thirst, cold and nakedness, and at length was fastened to the cruel cross that He might suffer the wrath of God in our behalf. These two things are sweet before the Most High; and for the sake of His doing and His dying, His substitutionary sufferings and His vicarious obedience, the Lord our God accepts us.

AUGUST 13.

*A*S the Father loves the Son, in the same manner Jesus loves His people. He loved Him *without beginning,* and thus Jesus loves us. *"I have loved thee with an everlasting love."* You can trace the beginning of human affection; you can easily find the beginning of your love to Christ, but His love to us is a stream whose source is hidden in eternity. God the Father loves Jesus *without any change.* Christian, take this for your comfort, that there is no change in Jesus Christ's love to those who rest in Him. Yesterday you were on the mount and you said, "He loves me:" to-day you are in the valley of humiliation, but He loves you still the same.

AUGUST 14.

And she said, Truth, Lord: yet the dogs eat of the crumbs which fall from their masters' table.—Matthew xv. 27.

*M*Y sins are many, but oh! it is nothing to Jesus to take them all away. "It will be but a small thing *for him* to give me full remission, although it will be an infinite blessing *for me* to receive it." The woman opens her soul wide, expecting great things of Jesus, and he fills it with his love. Dear reader, do the same. She laid fast hold upon him, drew arguments even out of his words; she believed great things of him, and she thus overcame him. SHE WON THE VICTORY BY BELIEVING IN HIM. Her case is an instance of prevailing faith; and if we would conquer like her, we must imitate her.

AUGUST 15.

*T*O whom belongest thou?" Reader, let me assist you in your response. *Have you been "born again"?* If you have, you belong to Christ; but without the new birth you cannot be his. *In whom do you trust?* For those who believe in Jesus are the sons of God. *Whose work are you doing?* You are sure to serve your master, for he whom you serve is thereby owned to be your lord. *What is your conversation?* Is it heavenly, or is it earthly? *What have you learned of your master?* If you have served your time with Jesus, it will be said of you, as it was of Peter and John, "They took knowledge of them that they had been with Jesus."

AUGUST 16.

*T*HE lives of some of God's people fill us with holy astonishment. Strange and marvelous are the ways which God used in their case to find his own. Blessed be his name, he never relinquishes the search until the chosen are sought out effectually. They are not a people sought to-day and cast away to-morrow. Almightiness and wisdom combined will make no failures; they shall be called *"Sought out!"* That any should be sought out, is matchless grace, but that *we* should be sought out is grace beyond degree! We can find no reason for it but God's own sovereign love, and can only lift up our heart in wonder, and praise the Lord that this day we wear the name of *"Sought out."*

AUGUST 17.

*W*E have sat at the table of the Lord's love, and said, "Nothing but the infinite can satisfy me; I am such a great sinner that I must have infinite merit to wash my sin away;" but we have had our sin removed, and found that there was merit to spare; we have had our hunger relieved at the feast of sacred love, and found that there was a redundance of spiritual meat remaining. Yes, there are graces to which we have not attained; places of fellowship nearer to Christ which we have not reached; and heights of communion which our feet have not climbed. At every banquet of love there are many baskets of fragments left. Let us magnify the liberality of our glorious Redeemer.

AUGUST 18.

*W*EARIED out with her wanderings, the dove returns at length to the ark as her only resting place. Noah has been looking out for his dove all day long, and is ready to receive her. She has just strength to reach the edge of the ark, when Noah puts forth his hand and pulls her in unto him. She did not fly right in herself, but was too fearful, or too weary, to do so. She flew as far as she could, and then he put forth his hand and pulled her in unto him. Just as she was she was pulled into the ark. So you, seeking sinner, with all your sin, will be received. "Only return"—these are God's two gracious words—"only return."

AUGUST 19.

AT this hour the church expects to walk in sympathy with her Lord along a thorny road; through much tribulation she is forcing her way to the crown. To bear the cross is her office, and yet the church has a deep well of joy, of which none can drink but her own children. There are stores of wine, and oil, and corn, hidden in the midst of our Jerusalem, upon which the saints of God are evermore sustained and nurtured; and sometimes, as in our Saviour's case, we have our seasons of intense delight, for "There is a river, the streams whereof shall make glad the city of our God." Exiles though we be, we rejoice in our King; yea, in him we exceedingly rejoice.

AUGUST 20.

THE Father loves the Son *without any end,* and thus does the Son love his people. Rest confident that even down to the grave Christ will go with you, and that up again from it he will be your guide to the celestial hills. Moreover, the Father loves the Son *without any measure,* and the same immeasurable love the Son bestows upon his chosen ones. The whole heart of Christ is dedicated to his people. He "loved us and gave himself for us." His is a love which passeth knowledge. Ah! we have indeed a precious Saviour, one who loves without measure, without change, without beginning, without end. even as the Father loves him!

AUGUST 21.

A LITTLE stay on earth will make heaven more heavenly. Nothing makes rest so sweet as toil. Our battered armor and scarred countenances will render more illustrious our victory above, when we are welcomed to the seats of those who have overcome the world. We should not have full *fellowship with Christ* if we did not for a while sojourn below, for he was baptized with a baptism of suffering among men, and we must be baptized with the same if we would share his kingdom. Fellowship with Christ is so honorable that the sorest sorrow is a light price by which to procure it.

AUGUST 22.

*D*IVINE omniscience affords no comfort to the ungodly mind, but to the child of God it overflows with consolation. God is always thinking upon us never turns aside his mind from us, for it would be dreadful to exist for a moment beyond the observation of our heavenly Father. His thoughts are always tender, loving, far-reaching, and they bring to us countless benefits. The Lord always did think upon his people: hence their election and the covenant of grace by which their salvation is secured; he always will think upon them: hence their final perseverance by which they shall be brought safely to their final rest.

AUGUST 23.

*I*F, trained by the Great Teacher, we follow where he leads, we shall find good, even while in this dark abode. But where shall this wisdom be found? Many have dreamed of it, but have not possessed it. Where shall we learn it? Let us listen to the voice of the Lord, for he hath declared the secret; he hath revealed to the sons of men wherein true wisdom lieth, and we have in it the text, "Whoso trusteth in the Lord, happy is he." *The true way to handle a matter wisely is to trust in the Lord.* This is the sure clue to the most intricate labyrinths of life. Lord, in this sweet eventide walk with me in the garden, and teach me the wisdom of faith.

AUGUST 24.

*I*T is well for us when prayers about our sorrows are linked wtih pleas concerning our sins —when, being under God's hand, we are not wholly taken up with our pain, but remember our offences against God. It is well, also to take both sorrow and sin to the same place. It was to God that David carried his sorrow: it was to God that David confessed his sin. Observe, then, *we must take our sorrows to God.* Even your little sorrows you may roll upon God, for he counteth the hairs of your head; and your great sorrows you may commit to him, for he holdeth the ocean in the hollow of his hand

AUGUST 25.

*P*RAYER sometimes tarrieth like a petitioner at the gate, until the King cometh forth to fill her bosom with the blessings which she seeketh. The Lord, when he hath given great faith, has been known to try it by long delayings. He has suffered his servants' voices to echo in their ears as from a brazen sky. Unanswered petitions are not unheard. By and by thy suit shall prevail. Canst thou not be content to wait a little? Will not thy Lord's time be better than thy time? By and by he will comfortably appear, to thy soul's joy, and make thee put away the sackcloth and ashes of long waiting, and put on the scarlet and fine linen of full fruition.

AUGUST 26.

*I*N all our wanderings the watchful glance of the Eternal Watcher is evermore fixed upon us— we never roam beyond the Shepherd's eye. In our sorrows he observes us incessantly, and not a pang escapes him; in our toils he marks all our weariness, and writes in his book all the struggles of his faithful ones. These thoughts of the Lord encompass us in all our paths, and penetrate the innermost region of our being.

Dear reader, is this precious to you? then hold to it. The Lord liveth and thinketh upon us, this is a truth far too precious for us to be lightly robbed of it. If the Lord thinketh upon us, all is well, and we may rejoice evermore.

AUGUST 27.

*B*EHOLD the epitaph of all those blessed saints who fell asleep before the coming of our Lord! It matters nothing how else they died, this one point, in which they all agree, is the most worthy of record, "they all died in faith." In faith they lived—it was their comfort, their guide, their motive, and their support; and in the same spiritual grace they died, ending their life-song in the sweet strain in which they had so long continued. They did not die resting in the flesh or upon their own attainments; they made no advance from their first way of acceptance with God, but held to the way of faith to the end.

AUGUST 28.

*W*E are so little, that if God should manifest his greatness without condescension, we should be trampled under his feet; but God, who must stoop to view the skies, and bow to see what angels do, turns his eye yet lower, and looks to the lowly and contrite, and makes them great.

"Thy gentleness hath made me great." How marvelous has been our experience of God's gentleness! How gentle have been his corrections! How gentle his teachings! How gentle his drawings! Meditate upon this theme, O believer. Let gratitude be awakened; let humility be deepened; let love be quickened, ere this day close.

AUGUST 29.

HOW independent of outward circumstances the Holy Ghost can make the Christian! What a bright light may shine within us when it is all dark without! How firm, how happy, how calm, how peaceful we may be, when the world shakes to and fro, and the pillars of the earth are removed! Even death itself, with all its terrible influences, has no power to suspend the music of a Christian's heart, but rather makes that music become more sweet, more clear, more heavenly, till the last kind act which death can do is to let the earthly strain melt into the heavenly chorus, the temporal joy into the eternal bliss!

AUGUST 30.

OUR Lord Jesus, by his death, did not purchase a right to a *part* of us only, but to the *entire* man. He contemplated in his passion the sanctification of us wholly, spirit, soul, and body. It is the business of the new-born nature which God has given to the regenerate to assert the rights of the Lord Jesus Christ. My soul, so far as thou art a child of God, thou must conquer all the rest of thyself which yet remains unblest; thou must subdue all thy powers and passions to the silver scepter of Jesus' gracious reign, and thou must never be satisfied till he who is king by purchase becomes also king by gracious coronation and reigns in thee supreme.

*W*ISDOM is man's true strength; and, under its guidance, he best accomplishes the ends of his being. Wisely handling the matter of life, gives to man the richest enjoyment, and presents the noblest occupation for his powers; hence by it he finds good in the fullest sense. Without wisdom, man is as the wild ass's colt, running hither and thither, wasting strength which might be profitably employed. Wisdom is the compass by which man is to steer across the trackless waste of life; without it he is a derelict vessel, the sport of winds and waves. A man must be prudent in such a world as this, or he will find no good, but be betrayed into unnumbered ills.

SEPTEMBER 1.

*I*T is easy work to pray when we are grounded, as to our desires, upon God's own promise. How can he that gave the word refuse to keep it? Immutable veracity cannot demean itself by a lie, and eternal faithfulness cannot degrade itself by neglect. God must bless His Son, his covenant binds him to it. That which the Spirit prompts us to ask for Jesus, is that which God decrees to give Him. Whenever you are praying for the kingdom of Christ, let your eyes behold the dawning of the blessed day which draweth near, when the Crucified shall receive His coronation in the place where men rejected him.

SEPTEMBER 2.

*I*F we fear the Lord, we may look for timely interpositions when our case is at its worst. Angels are not kept from us by storms, or hindered by darkness. Seraphs think it no humiliation to visit the poorest of the heavenly family. If angels' visits are few and far between at ordinary times, they shall be frequent in our nights of tempest and tossing.

Dear reader, is this an hour of distress with you? Then ask for peculiar help. Jesus is the angel of the covenant, and if his presence be now earnestly sought, it will not be denied. What that presence brings is heart cheer.

SEPTEMBER 3.

DYING in faith has distinct reference to *the past*. They believed the promises which had gone before, and were assured that their sins were blotted out through the mercy of God. Dying in faith has to do with the present. These saints were confident of their acceptance with God, they enjoyed the beams of His love, and rested in His faithfulness. Dying in faith looks into *the future*. They fell asleep, affirming that the Messiah would surely come. Thy course, through grace, is one of faith, and sight seldom cheers thee: this has also been the pathway of the brightest and the best.

SEPTEMBER 4.

IT is exceedingly beneficial to our souls to mount above this present evil world to something nobler and better. It would be well if the dwellers in the valley could frequently leave their abodes among the marshes and the fever mists, and inhale the bracing element upon the hills. It is to such an exploit of climbing that I now invite you. May the Spirit of God assist us to leave the mists of fear and the fevers of anxiety, and all the ills which gather in this valley of earth, and to ascend the mountains of anticipated joy and blessedness. May God the Holy Spirit cut the cords that keep us here below, and assist us to mount.

SEPTEMBER 5.

*B*E courageous concerning this, O Christian! be not dispirited, as though your spiritual enemies could never be destroyed; thou art Christ's, and sin has no right to thee.

You are able to overcome them—not in your own strength—the weakest of them would be too much for you in that; but you can and shall overcome them through the blood of the Lamb. Do not ask, "How shall I dispossess them, for they are greater and mightier than I?" But go to the strong for strength, wait humbly upon God, and the mighty God of Jacob will surely come to the rescue, and you shall sing of victory through His grace.

SEPTEMBER 6.

*T*O this man will I look, even to him that is poor and of a contrite spirit, and trembleth at My word." Stoop if you would climb to heaven. Do we not say of Jesus, "He descended that He might ascend?" So must you. You must grow downwards, that you may grow upwards; for the sweetest fellowship with heaven is to be had by humble souls, and by them alone. God will deny no blessing to a thoroughly humbled spirit. Humility makes us ready to be blessed by the God of all grace, and fits us to deal efficiently with our fellow-men. Whether it be prayer or praise, whether it be work or suffering, the genuine salt of humility cannot be used in excess.

HALLOWED be thy name; thy kingdom come; thy will be done in earth as it is in heaven." Let not your prayers be all concerning your own sins, your own wants, your own imperfections, your own trials, but let them climb the starry ladder, and get up to Christ himself, and then, as you draw nigh to the blood-besprinkled mercy-seat, offer this prayer continually, "Lord, extend the kingdom of thy dear Son." Such a petition, fervently presented, will elevate the spirit of all your devotions. Mind that you prove the sincerity of your prayer by laboring to promote the Lord's glory.

SEPTEMBER 8.

SEARCH the Scriptures." The Greek word here rendered *search* signifies a strict, close, diligent search, such as men make when they are seeking gold, or hunters when they are in earnest after game. We must not rest content with having given a superficial reading to a chapter or two, but with the candle of the Spirit we must deliberately seek out the hidden meaning of the word. Holy Scripture *requires searching*—much of it can only be learned by careful study. No man who merely skims the book of God can profit thereby; we must dig and mine until we obtain the hid treasure. The Scriptures *claim searching*.

SEPTEMBER 9.

"*THE Lord is my light and my salvation.*" Here is personal interest, "*my light,*" "*my salvation;*" the soul is assured of it, and therefore declares it boldly. Into the soul at the new birth divine light is poured as the precursor of salvation. Where there is not enough light to reveal our own darkness, and to make us long for the Lord Jesus, there is no evidence of salvation. After conversion our God is our joy, comfort, guide, teacher, and in every sense our light: he is light within, light around, light reflected from us, and light to be revealed to us. He, then, who by faith has laid hold upon God, has all covenant blessings in his possession.

SEPTEMBER 10.

*S*URELY if there be a happy verse in the Bible, it is this—"My Beloved is mine, and I am his." So peaceful, so full of assurance, so overrunning with happiness and contentment is it, that it might well have been written by the same hand which penned the twenty-third Psalm. The verse savors of him who, an hour before he went to Gethsemane, said, "Peace I leave with you, my peace I give unto you: not as the world giveth, give I unto you." "In the world ye shall have tribulation: but be of good cheer; I have overcome the world." Let us ring the silver bell again, for its notes are exquisitely sweet: "My Beloved is mine, and I am his."

SEPTEMBER 11.

*N*O Christian is safe when his soul is slothful, and his God is far from him. Every Christian is always safe as to the great matter of his standing in Christ, but he is not safe as regards his experience in holiness, and communion with Jesus in this life. Satan does not often attack a Christian who is living near God. It is when the Christian departs from his God, becomes spiritually starved, and endeavors to feed on vanities, that the devil discovers his vantage hour. He may sometimes stand foot to foot with the child of God who is active in his Master's service, but the battle is generally short. Oh for grace to walk humbly with our God!

SEPTEMBER 12.

*H*E *draws us to closer communion with himself*. We have been sitting on the doorstep of God's house, and he bids us advance into the banqueting hall and sup with him, but we decline the honor. There are secret rooms not yet opened to us; Jesus invites us to enter them, but we hold back. Shame on our cold hearts! We are but poor lovers of our sweet Lord Jesus, not fit to be his servants, much less to be his brides, and yet he hath exalted us to be bone of his bone, and flesh of his flesh, married to him by a glorious marriage covenant Herein is love!

SEPTEMBER 13.

*H*OW blessed to feel assured that the Lord is with us in all our ways, and condescends to go down into our humiliations and banishments with us! Even beyond the ocean our Father's love beams like the sun in its strength. We cannot hesitate to go where Jehovah promises his presence. *"Fear not,"* is the Lord's command and his divine encouragement to those who at his bidding are launching upon new seas; the divine presence and preservation forbid so much as one unbelieving fear. Without our God we should fear to move; but when he bids us go it would be dangerous to tarry. Reader, go forward, and fear not.

SEPTEMBER 14.

*T*HE love which the early Christians felt towards the Lord was not a quiet emotion which they hid within themselves in the secret chamber of their souls, and which they only spake of when they met on the first day of the week, and sang hymns in honor of Christ Jesus the crucified, but it was a passion with them of such a vehement and all-consuming energy, that it was visible in their actions, spoke in their common talk, and looked out of their eyes even in their commonest glances. Love to Jesus was a flame which fed upon the core and heart of their being; and, therefore, from its own force burned its way into the outer man, and shone there.

SEPTEMBER 15.

*L*OOK at thy possessions, O believer, and compare thy portion with the lot of thy fellow-men. Some of them have their portion in the field; they are rich and their harvests yield them a golden increase; but what are harvests compared with thy God, who is the God of harvests? What are bursting granaries compared with him, who is the Husbandman, and feeds thee with the bread of heaven? Some have their portion in the city; their wealth is abundant, and flows to them in constant streams, until they become a very reservoir of gold; but what is gold compared with thy God? *"Thou art my portion, O Lord."*—Psalm cxix.

SEPTEMBER 16.

*J*ESUS is the great teacher of lowliness of heart. We need daily to learn of him. See the Master taking a towel and washing his disciples' feet! Follower of Christ, wilt thou not humble thyself? See him as the Servant of servants, and surely thou canst not be proud! "He humbled himself!" Was he not on earth always stripping off first one robe of honor, and then another, till, naked, he was fastened to the cross? and there did he not empty out his inmost self, pouring out his life-blood, giving up for all us? How low was our dear Redeemer brought! How then, can we be proud?

SEPTEMBER 17.

We would see Jesus.—John xii. 21.

IS this thy condition, my reader, at this moment? Hast thou but one desire, and is that after Christ? Then thou art not far from the kingdom of heaven. Hast thou but one wish in thy heart, and that one wish that thou mayest be washed from all thy sins in Jesus' blood? Canst thou really say, "I would give all I have to be a Christian; I would give up everything I have and hope for, if I might but feel that I have an interest in Christ?" Then, despite all thy fears, be of good cheer, the Lord loveth thee, and thou shalt come out into daylight soon, and rejoice in the liberty wherewith Christ makes men free.

SEPTEMBER 18.

JESUS gave his blood for us; what shall we give to him? We are his, and all that we have, for he has purchased us into himself—can we act as if we were our own? Oh for more consecration! and to this end, oh for more love! Blessed Jesus, thou dost receive with favor the smallest sincere token of affection! Thou dost receive our poor forget-me-nots and love-tokens, as though they were intrinsically precious, though indeed they are but as the bunch of wild flowers which the child brings to its mother. We will give thee the first fruits of our increase, and pay thee tithes of all, and then we will confess "of thine own have we given thee."

SEPTEMBER 19.

*W*E have each of us peculiar gifts and special manifestations; but the one object God has in view is, the perfecting of the whole body of Christ. We must, therefore, bring our spiritual possessions and lay them at the apostles' feet, and make distribution unto all of what God has given to us. Keep back no part of the precious truth, but speak what you know, and testify what you have seen. Let not the toil, or darkness, or possible unbelief of your friends, weigh one moment in the scale. Up, and be marching to the place of duty, and there tell what great things God has shown to your soul. We too must bear our witness concerning Jesus.

SEPTEMBER 20.

*I*T is well with the righteous—*well upon divine authority;* the mouth of God speaks the comforting assurance. Blessed be God for a faith which enables us to believe God when the creatures contradict him. It is, says the word, at all times well with thee, thou righteous one; then, beloved, if thou canst not see it, let God's word stand thee in stead of sight; yea, believe it on divine authority more confidently than if thine eyes and thy feeling told it to thee. Whom God blesses is blest indeed, and what his lip declares is truth most sure and steadfast

SEPTEMBER 21.

*J*ESUS wears all the glory which the pomp of heaven can bestow upon him, which ten thousand times ten thousand angels can minister to him. You cannot with your utmost stretch of imagination conceive his exceeding greatness: yet there will be a further revelation of it when he shall descend from heaven in great power, with all the holy angels—"Then shall he sit upon the throne of his glory." Oh, the splendor of that glory! Nor is this the close, for eternity shall sound his praise. "Thy throne, O God, is forever and ever!" Reader, if you would joy in Christ's glory hereafter, he must be glorious in your sight now. *Is he so?*

SEPTEMBER 22.

*W*HEN the two disciples had reached Emmaus, and were refreshing themselves at the evening meal, the mysterious stranger who had so enchanted them upon the road, took bread and brake it, made himself known to them, and then vanished out of their sight. They had constrained him to abide with them, because the day was far spent; but now, although it was much later, their love was a lamp to their feet, yea, wings also; they forgot the darkness, their weariness was all gone, and forthwith they journeyed back the threescore furlongs to tell the gladsome news of a risen Lord, who had appeared to them by the way.

SEPTEMBER 23.

*G*OD neither chose us nor called us because we were holy, but he called us that we might be holy, and holiness is the beauty produced by his workmanship in us. The excellencies which we see in a believer are as much the work of God as the atonement itself. Thus is brought out very sweetly the fullness of the grace of God. Salvation must be of grace, because the Lord is the author of it. Salvation must be of grace, because the Lord works in such a manner that our righteousness is forever excluded. Such is the believer's privilege—*a present salvation;* such is the evidence that he is called to it—*a holy life.*

SEPTEMBER 24.

*B*ELIEVER, do you remember that rapturous day when you first realized pardon through Jesus the sin-bearer? Can you not make glad confession, and say, "My soul recalls her day of deliverance with delight. Laden with guilt and full of fears, I saw my Saviour as my Substitute, and I laid my hand upon him; oh! how timidly at first, but courage grew, and confidence was confirmed, until I leaned my soul entirely upon him; and now it is my unceasing joy to know that my sins are no longer imputed to me, but laid upon him, and like the debts of the wounded traveller, Jesus, like the good Samaritan, has said of all my future sinfulness, 'Set that to my account.'"

SEPTEMBER 25.

*D*OST thou think, O Christian, that thou canst measure the love of Christ? Think of what His love has brought thee—justification, adoption, sanctification, eternal life! The riches of His goodness are unsearchable! Oh, the breadth of the love of Christ! Shall such a love as this have half our hearts? Shall Jesus' marvelous loving-kindness and tender care meet with but faint response and tardy acknowledgment? O my soul, tune thy heart to a glad song of thanksgiving! Go through the day rejoicing, for thou art no desolate wanderer, but a beloved child, watched over, cared for, supplied, and defended by thy Lord.

SEPTEMBER 26.

*E*NDEAVOR to know *the Father,* bury your head in his bosom in deep repentance, and confess that you are not worthy to be called his son; receive the kiss of his love; let the ring which is the token of his eternal faithfulness be on your finger; sit at his table and let your heart make merry in his grace. Then press forward and seek to know much of *the Son* of God; know him as eternal God, and yet suffering, finite man; follow him as he walks the waters with the tread of deity, and as he sits upon the well in the weariness of humanity. Be not satisfied unless you know much of Jesus Christ as your Friend, your Brother, your Husband, your all.

SEPTEMBER 27.

*A*ND he is full of truth. True have his promises been; not one has failed. I want none beside him. In life he is my life, and in death he shall be the death of death; in poverty Christ is my riches; in sickness he makes my bed; in darkness he is my star, and in brightness he is my sun; He is the manna of the camp in the wilderness, and he shall be the new corn of the host when they come to Canaan. Jesus is to me all grace and no wrath, all truth and no falsehood: and of truth and grace he is *full,* infinitely full. My soul, this day, bless with all thy might "the only Begotten."

SEPTEMBER 28.

*H*OW comprehensive is the love of Jesus! There is no part of his people's interests which he does not consider, and there is nothing which concerns their welfare which is not important to him. "The steps of a good man are ordered by the Lord: and he delighteth in his way." Believer, rest assured that the heart of Jesus cares about your meaner affairs. The breadth of his tender love is such that you may resort to him in all matters; for in all your afflictions he is afflicted, and like as a father pitieth his children, so doth he pity you. The meanest interests of all his saints are all borne upon the broad bosom of the Son of God.

SEPTEMBER 29.

*O*UR God's tender love for his servants makes him concerned for the state of their inward feelings. He desires them to be of good courage. Some esteem it a small thing for a believer to be vexed with doubts and fears, but God thinks not so. Our Master does not think so lightly of our unbelief as we do. Our Lord loveth not to see our countenance sad. It was a law of Ahasuerus, that no one should come into the king's court dressed in mourning; this is not the law of the King of kings, for we may come mourning as we are; but still he would have us put off the spirit of heaviness, and put on the garment of praise, for there is much reason to rejoice.

SEPTEMBER 30.

*I*F his dark nights are as bright as the world's days, what shall his days be? If even his starlight is more splendid than the sun, what must his sunlight be? If he can praise the Lord in the fires, how will he extol him before the eternal throne! If evil be good to him *now,* what will the overflowing goodness of God be to him *then?* Oh, blessed "afterward!" Who would not be a Christian? Who would not bear the present cross for the crown which cometh afterwards? But herein is work for patience, for the rest is not for to-day, nor the triumph for the present, but "afterward." Wait, O soul, and let patience have her perfect work.

OCTOBER 1.

*W*HAT is your desire this day? Is it set upon heavenly things? Do you desire liberty in close communication with God? Do you aspire to know the heights, and depths, and lengths, and breadths? Then you must draw near to Jesus; you must get a clear sight of him in his preciousness and completeness. He who understands Christ, receives an anointing from the Holy One, by which he knows all things. Are you saying, "O that he would dwell in my bosom?" "Would that he would make my heart his dwelling-place forever?" Open the door, beloved, and he will come into your souls. He has long been knocking, and he will sup with you, and you with him.

OCTOBER 2.

*P*OOR souls! forget not the present Saviour, who bids you look unto him and be saved. *He* could heal you at once, but you prefer to wait for an angel and a wonder. To trust him is a sure way to every blessing, and he is worthy of the most implicit confidence; but unbelief makes you prefer the cold porches of Bethesda to the warm bosom of his love. O that the Lord may turn his eye upon the multitudes who are in this case to-day; may he forgive the slights which they have put upon his divine power, and call them by that sweet constraining voice, to rise from the bed of despair, and in the energy of faith take up their bed and walk.

OCTOBER 3.

*C*HRISTIANS are not to be praised for neglected duties under the pretense of having secret fellowship with Jesus: it is not sitting, but *sitting at Jesus' feet,* which is commendable. Do not think that activity is in itself an evil: it is a great blessing and a means of grace to us. Those who have most fellowship with Christ are not recluses or hermits, but indefatigable laborers who are toiling for Jesus, and who, in their toil, have him side by side with them, so that they are workers together with God. Let us remember, then, in anything we have to do for Jesus, that we can do it, and should do it, in close communion with him.

OCTOBER 4.

*W*E must manifest the spirit of Christ in meekness, gentleness, and forgiveness. Let us search and see if we truly *suffer with Jesus.* And if we do thus suffer, what is our "light affliction" compared with *reigning with him?* Oh, it is so blessed to be in the furnace with Christ, and such an honor to stand in the pillory with him, that if there were no future reward, we might count ourselves happy in present honor; but when the recompense is so eternal, so infinitely more than we had any right to expect, shall we not take up the cross with alacrity, and go on our way rejoicing?

OCTOBER 5.

*H*E has been good to me in all my needs, trials, struggles, and sorrows. Never could there be a better Master, for his service is freedom, his rule is love. The ancient saints proved him to be a good Master, and each of them rejoiced to sing, "I am thy servant, O Lord!" I will bear this witness before my friends and neighbors, for possibly they may be led by my testimony to seek my Lord Jesus as their Master. Oh that they would do so! They would never repent so wise a deed. If they would but take his easy yoke, they would find themselves in so royal a service that they would enlist in it forever.

OCTOBER 6.

*M*Y soul, hearken to the voice of thy God. He is always ready to speak with thee when thou art prepared to hear. If there be any slowness to commune, it is not on his part, but altogether on thine own; for he stands at the door and knocks, and if his people will but open, he rejoices to enter. But in what state is my heart, which is my Lord's garden? May I venture to hope that it is bringing forth fruit fit for him? If not, he will have much to reprove; but still I pray him to come unto me, for nothing can so certainly bring my heart into a right condition as the presence of the Sun of Righteousness, who brings healing in his wings.

OCTOBER 7.

HE sups with you because you find the house or the heart, and *you with him* because he brings the provision. He could not sup with you if it were not in your heart; nor could you sup with him if he did not bring the provision with him. Fling wide, then, the portals of your soul. He will come with that love which you long to feel; he will come with that joy into which you cannot work your poor depressed spirit; he will bring the peace which now you have not. Only open the door to him, and he will dwell there forever. Oh, wondrous love, that brings such a guest to dwell in such a heart!

OCTOBER 8.

*F*AITH in Jesus is more than a match for worldly trials, temptations, unbelief, and overcomes them all. The same absorbing principle shines in the faithful service of God; with an enthusiastic love for Jesus, difficulties are surmounted, sacrifices become pleasures, sufferings are honors. But if religion is thus a consuming passion in the heart, then it follows that there are many persons who profess religion, but have it not; for what they have will not bear this test. Examine yourself, my reader, on this point. Aaron's rod *proved* its heaven-given power. Is your religion doing so? If Christ be anything, he must be everything. Oh, rest not till love and faith in Jesus be the master passions of your soul!

OCTOBER 9.

*I*T *is well wtih the righteous* ALWAYS. From the beginning of the year to the end of the year, from the first gathering of evening shadows until the day-star shines, in all conditions, and under all circumstances, it shall be well with the righteous. It is so well with him that we could not imagine it to be better, for he is *well fed,* he feeds upon the flesh and blood of Jesus; he is *well clothed,* he wears the imputed righteousness of Christ; he is *well housed,* he dwells in God; he is *well married,* his soul is knit in bonds of marriage union to Christ; he is *well provided for,* for the Lord is his Shepherd; he is *well endowed,* for heaven is his inheritance.

OCTOBER 10.

*S*HOULD it happen that, in the providence of God, you are a loser by conscience, you shall find that if the Lord pays you not back in the silver of earthly prosperity, he will discharge his promise in the gold of spiritual joy. Remember that a man's life consisteth not in the abundance of that which he possesseth. To wear a guileless spirit, to have a heart void of offence, to have the favor and smile of God, is greater riches than the mines of Ophir could yield, or the traffic of Tyre could win. "Better is a dinner of herbs where love is, than a stalled ox and inward contention therewith." An ounce of heart's-ease is worth a ton of gold.

OCTOBER 11.

WE must not imagine that we are suffering for Christ, and with Christ, if we are not in Christ. Beloved friend, are you trusting to Jesus only? If not, whatever you may have to mourn over on earth, you are not "suffering with Christ," and have no hope of regaining with him in heaven. Neither are we to conclude that all a Christian's sufferings are sufferings with Christ, for *it is essential that he be called by God to suffer.* If we are rash and imprudent, and run into positions for which neither providence nor grace has fitted us, we ought to question whether we are not rather sinning than communing with Jesus.

OCTOBER 12.

COME, O Lord my God; my soul invites thee earnestly, and waits for thee eagerly. Come to me, O Jesus, my well beloved, and plant fresh flowers in my garden, such as I see blooming in such perfection in thy matchless character! Come, O my Father, who art the Husbandman, and deal with me in thy tenderness and prudence! Come, O Holy Spirit, and bedew my whole nature, as the herbs are now moistened with the evening dews. Oh, that God would speak to me! Speak, Lord, for thy servant heareth. Oh, that he would walk with me; I am ready to give up my whole heart and mind to him. I am only asking what he delights to give.

OCTOBER 13.

GOD is glorified by our serving him in our proper vocations. Every lawful trade may be sanctified by the gospel to noblest ends. Turn to the Bible, and you will find the most menial forms of labor connected either with most daring deeds of faith, or with persons whose lives have been illustrious for holiness. Therefore be not discontented with your calling. Whatever God has made your position, or your work, abide in that, unless you are *quite sure* that he calls you to something else. Let your first care be to glorify God to the utmost of your power where you are. Fill your present sphere to his praise, and if he needs you in another he will show it you.

OCTOBER 14.

NO human mind can adequately estimate the infinite value of the divine sacrifice, for great as is the sin of God's people, the atonement which takes it away is immeasurably greater. Therefor the believer, even when sin rolls like a black flood, and the remembrance of the past is bitter, can yet stand before the blazing throne of the great and holy God, and cry, "Who is he that condemneth? It is Christ that died; yea, rather, that hath risen again." While the recollection of his sin fills him with shame and sorrow, he at the same time makes it a foil to show the brightness of mercy—guilt is the dark night in which the fair star of divine love shines with serene splendor.

OCTOBER 15.

IT is a happy thing when we can address the Lord with the confidence which David manifests; it gives us great power in prayer, and comfort in trial. *"On thee do I wait all the day."* Patience is the fair handmaid and daughter of faith; we cheerfully wait when we are certain that we shall not wait in vain. It is our duty and our privilege to wait upon the Lord in service, in worship, in expectancy, in trust, all the days of our life. Our faith will be tried faith, and if it be of the true kind, it will bear continued trial without yielding. We shall not grow weary of waiting upon God if we remember how long and how graciously he once waited for us.

OCTOBER 16.

SEEING that we have such a God to trust to, let us rest upon him with all our weight; let us resolutely drive out all unbelief, and endeavor to get rid of doubts and fears, which so much mar our comfort; since there is no excuse for fear where God is the foundation of our trust. A loving parent would be sorely grieved if his child could not trust him; and how ungenerous, how unkind is our conduct when we put so little confidence in our heavenly Father, who has never failed us, and who never will! We have been in many trials, but we have never yet been cast where we could not find in our God all that we needed.

OCTOBER 17.

"He appeared first to Mary Magdalene."—Mark 16:9.

IF we would see much of Christ, let us *serve* him Tell me who they are that sit oftenest under the banner of his love, and drink deepest draughts from the cup of communion, and I am sure they will be those who give most, who serve best, and who abide closest to the bleeding heart of their dear Lord. But notice *how* Christ revealed himself to this sorrowing one—by *a word*, "Mary." It needed but one word *in his voice,* and at once she knew him, and *her heart owned allegiance by another word,* her heart was too full to say more. That one word most fitting. It implies obedience. She said *"Master."*

OCTOBER 18.

CHRISTIAN man! learn to comfort thyself in God's gracious dealing toward the church. That which is so dear to thy Master, should it not be dear above all else to thee? What though thy way be dark, canst thou not gladden thine heart with the triumphs of his cross and the spread of his truth? Our own personal troubles are forgotten while we look, not only upon what God *has* done, and *is* doing for Zion, but on the glorious things he *will yet do* for his church. Try this receipt, O believer, whenever thou art sad of heart and in heaviness of spirit: "Pray for the peace of Jerusalem," and thine own soul shall be refreshed.

OCTOBER 19.

*G*OD is for me." He was "for us" or he would not have given his well beloved Son. And because he is "for us," the voice of prayer will always insure his help. *"When I cry unto thee, then shall mine enemies be turned back."* This is no uncertain hope, but a well-grounded assurance— *"this I know."* I will direct my prayer unto thee, and will look up for the answer, assured that it will come, "for God is for me." O believer, how happy art thou with the King of kings on thy side. How safe with such a Protector! How sure thy cause, pleaded by such an Advocate! If God be for thee, who can be against thee?

OCTOBER 20.

*T*HE blood of Jesus Christ his Son cleanseth us from *all sin"* not only from sin, but "from *all* sin." Reader, I cannot tell you the exceeding sweetness of this word, but I pray God the Holy Ghost to give you a taste of it. Manifold are our sins against God. Whether the bill be little or great, the same receipt can discharge one as the other. The blood of Jesus Christ is as blessed and divine a payment for the transgressions of blaspheming Peter as for the shortcomings of loving John; our iniquity is gone, all gone at once, and all gone forever. Blessed completeness! What a sweet theme to dwell upon as one begins another day.

A TRUE believer, called by grace and washed in the precious blood of Jesus, thou hast tasted of better drink than the river of this world's pleasure can give thee; thou hast had fellowship with Christ; thou hast obtained the joy of seeing Jesus, and leaning thine head upon His bosom. Do the trifles, the songs, the honors, the merriment of this earth content thee after that? If thou art wandering after the waters of Egypt, oh, return quickly to the one living fountain: the waters of Sihor may be sweet to the Egyptians, but they will prove only bitterness to thee. What hast *thou to do with them? Jesus asks thee this question*—what wilt thou answer Him?

OCTOBER 22.

"Why go I mourning?"—Psalm xlii. 9.

C ANST thou answer this, believer? Can't thou find any reason why thou art so often mourning instead of rejoicing? Why yield to gloomy anticipations? Who told thee that the night would never end in day? Who told thee that the winter of thy discontent would proceed from frost to frost, from snow and ice, and hail, to deeper snow, and yet more heavy tempest of despair? Knowest thou not that day follows night, that flood comes after ebb, that spring and summer succeed to winter? Hope thou then! Hope thou ever! for God fails thee not.

OCTOBER 23.

*I*F there be one place where our Lord Jesus most fully becomes the joy and comfort of His people, it is where He plunged deepest into the depths of woe. Come hither, gracious souls, and behold the Man in the garden of Gethsemane; behold His heart so brimming with love that He cannot hold it in—so full of sorrow that it must find a vent. Behold the Man as they drive the nails into His hands and feet. Look up, repenting sinners, and see the sorrowful image of your suffering Lord. If we would live aright, it must be by the contemplation of His death; if we would rise to dignity, it must be by considering His humiliation and His sorrow.

OCTOBER 24.

*W*HO can lay anything to the charge of God's Elect?" Most blessed challenge! How unanswerable it is! Every sin of the elect was laid upon the great Champion of our salvation, and by the atonement carried away. There is no sin in God's book against His people. When the guilt of sin was taken away, the punishment of sin was removed. For the Christian there is no stroke from God's angry hand—nay, not so much as a single frown of justice. The believer may be chastised by his Father, but God the Judge has nothing to say to the Christian, except "I have absolved thee: thou art acquitted."

OCTOBER 25.

And the evening and the morning were the first day."
Genesis i. 5.

*T*HE evening was "darkness" and the morning was "light," and yet *the two together are called by the name that is given to the light alone!* In every believer there is darkness and light, and yet he is not a sinner because there is sin in him, but he is a saint because he possesses some degree of holiness. This will be a most comforting thought to those who ask, "Can I be a child of God while there is so much darkness in me?" Yes; for you, like the day, take not your name from the evening, but from the morning; and you are spoken of in the word of God as if you were even now perfectly holy.

OCTOBER 26.

*O*F the Saviour, and only of the Saviour, is it true in the fullest, broadest, and most unqualified sense. "He went about doing good. From this description it is evident that He did good *personally.* The evangelists constantly tell us that He touched the leper with His own finger, that He anointed the eyes of the blind, and that in cases where He was asked to speak the word only at a distance, He did not usually comply, but went Himself to the sick bed, and there personally wrought the cure. A lesson to us, if he would do good, to do it ourselves. "He hath left us an example that we should follow in His steps."

OCTOBER 27.

I GIVE unto my sheep," saith he, "eternal life; and they shall never perish, neither shall any man pluck them out of my hand." What sayest thou to this, O trembling feeble mind? Is not this a precious mercy, that coming to Christ, thou dost not come to one who will treat thee well for a little while, and then send thee away, but he will receive thee and make thee his bride, and thou shalt be his forever. Receive no longer the spirit of bondage again to fear, but the spirit of adoption whereby thou shalt cry, Abba, Father! Oh, the grace of these words, "I will in no wise cast out!"

OCTOBER 28.

"Thou crownest the year with thy goodness."—Psalm lxv. 11

A LL the year round, every hour of every day, God is richly blessing us; both when we sleep and when we wake his mercy waits upon us. The sun may leave us a legacy of darkness, by our God never ceases to shine upon his children with beams of love. Like a river, his loving kindness is always flowing with a fullness inexhaustible as his own nature. Like the atmosphere which constantly surrounds the earth, and is always ready to support the life of man, the benevolence of God surrounds all his creatures; in it, as in their element, they live, and move, and have their being.

OCTOBER 29.

*I*F the most precious are tried in the fire, are we to escape the crucible? If the diamond must be vexed upon the wheel, are we to be made perfect without suffering? Who hath commanded the wind to cease from blowing because our bark is on the deep? Why and wherefore should we be treated better than our Lord? The First-born felt the rod, and why not the younger brethren? It is pride which would choose a downy pillow and a silken couch for a soldier of the cross. Wiser far is he who, being first resigned to the divine will, groweth by the energy of grace to be pleased with it, and so learns to gather lilies at the cross-foot, and, like Samson, to find honey in the lion.

OCTOBER 30.

*I*F our Lord is so ready to heal the sick and bless the needy, then, my soul, be not thou slow to put thyself in his way, that he may smile on thee. Be not slack in asking, if he be so abundant in bestowing. Give earnest heed to his word now, that Jesus may speak through it to thy heart. Where he is to be found, there make thy resort, that thou mayest obtain his blessing. When he is present to heal, may he not heal thee? But surely he is present even now, for he always comes to hearts which need him. And dost not thou need him? Ah, *he* knows how much! Thou Son of David, turn thine eye and look upon the distress which is now before thee and make thy suppliant whole.

OCTOBER 31.

"The Lord trieth the righteous."—Psalm xi. 5.

ALL events are under the control of Providence; consequently all the trials of our outward life are traceable at once to the great First Cause. All providences are doors to trials. Even our mercies, like roses, have their thorns. Our mountains are not too high, and our valleys are not too low, for temptations: trials lurk on all roads. Everywhere, above and beneath, we are beset and surrounded with dangers. Yet no shower falls unpermitted from the threatening cloud; every drop has its order ere it hastens to the earth. The trials which come from God are sent to prove and strengthen us.

NOVEMBER 1.

*L*ET me command to you a life of trust in God in temporal things. Walk in your path of integrity with steadfast steps, and show that you are invincibly strong in the strength which confidence in God alone can confer. Thus you will be delivered from carking care, you will not be troubled with evil tidings, your heart will be fixed, trusting in the Lord. How pleasant to float along the stream of providence! There is no more blessed way of living than a life of dependence upon a covenant-keeping God. We have no care, for he careth for us; we have no troubles, because we cast our burdens upon the Lord.

NOVEMBER 2.

*H*EAL my soul, for I have sinned against thee." For this also the godly praise the name of the Lord, saying, "He healeth all our diseases." What a transcendent comfort it is that in the person of Jesus "dwelleth all the fullness of the Godhead bodily!" My soul, whatever thy disease may be, this great Physician can heal thee. If He be God, there can be no limit to his power. Come just as thou art, for he who is God can certainly restore thee of thy plague. None shall restrain the healing virtue which proceeds from Jesu our Lord. All his patients have been cured in the past, and shall be in the future, and thou shalt be one among them, my friend, if thou wilt but rest thyself in him.

NOVEMBER 3.

"If we walk in the light, as he is in the light."—1 John i. 7

*A*S he is in the light! Can we ever attain to this? Shall we ever be able to walk as clearly in the light as he is whom we call "Our Father," of whom it is written, "God is light, and in him is no darkness at all?" Certainly, this is the model which is set before us, for the Saviour himself said, "Be ye perfect, even as your Father who is in heaven is perfect;" and although we may feel that we can never rival the perfection of God, yet we are to seek after it, and never be satisfied until we attain to it.

NOVEMBER 4.

*F*OR thou art my strength." What an inexpressible sweetness is to be found in these few words! How joyfully may we encounter toils, and how cheerfully may we endure sufferings, when we can lay hold upon celestial strength. He is a happy man who has such matchless might engaged upon his side. Our own strength would be of little service when embarrassed in the nets of base cunning, but the Lord's strength is ever available; we have but to invoke it, and we shall find it near at hand. If by faith we are depending alone upon the strength of the mighty God of Israel, we may use our holy reliance as a plea in supplication.

NOVEMBER 5.

*T*HOUGH we have brought forth some fruit unto Christ, and have a joyful hope that we are "plants of his own right hand planting," yet there are times when we feel very barren. Prayer is lifeless, love is cold, faith is weak, each grace in the garden of our heart languishes and droops. We are like flowers in the hot sun, requiring the refreshing shower. In such a condition what are we to do? *"Sing, O barren, break forth and cry aloud."* Sing, believer, for it will cheer thine own heart, and the hearts of other desolate ones. Sing on, for now that God makes thee *loth* to be without fruit he will soon cover thee with clusters.

NOVEMBER 6.

"Ourselves also, which have the first fruits of the Spirit."
Romans viii. 23.

*B*UT the first fruits were not the harvest, and the works of the Spirit in us at this moment, are not the consummation—the perfection is yet to come. We must not boast that we have attained, and so reckon the wave-sheaf to be all the produce of the year: we must hunger and thirst after righteousness, and pant for the day of full redemption. Dear reader, this day open your heart wide, and God will fill it. Groan within yourself for higher degrees of consecration, and your Lord will grant them to you, for he is able to do exceeding abundantly above what we ask, or even think.

NOVEMBER 7.

*G*OD makes no difference in his love to his children. A child is a child to him; he will not make him a hired servant; but he shall feast upon the fatted calf, and shall have the music and the dancing as much as if he had never gone astray. No chains are worn in the court of King Jesus. Our admission into full privileges may be gradual, but it is sure. Perhaps our reader is saying, "I wish I could enjoy the promises, and walk at liberty in my Lord's commands." "If thou believest with all thine heart, thou mayest." Loose the chains of thy neck, O captive daughter, for Jesus makes thee free.

NOVEMBER 8.

*T*O know Christ and be found in Him—oh, this is life, this is joy, this is marrow and fatness. *His unsearchable riches will be best known in eternity.* He will give you, on the way to heaven, all you need; your place of defense shall be the munitions of rocks, your bread shall be given you, and your waters shall be sure; but it is there, THERE, where you shall hear the song of them that triumph, the shout of them that feast, and shall see the glorious and beloved One. The unsearchable riches of Christ! Lord, teach us more and more of Jesus, and we will tell out the good news to others.

*B*EYOND measure it is desirable that we, as believers, should have the person of Jesus constantly before us, to inflame our love towards Him, and to increase our knowledge of Him. But to have Jesus ever near, the heart must be full of Him, welling up with His love, even to overrunning; hence the apostle prays "that Christ may *dwell in your hearts.*" See how near he would have Jesus to be! *"That He may dwell:"* not that He may call upon you sometimes, as a casual visitor enters into a house and tarries for a night, but that He may *dwell*, that Jesus may become the Lord and Tenant of your heart.

NOVEMBER 10.

*T*HE believer commits his soul to the hand of his God; it came from Him, it is His own, He has aforetime sustained it, He is able to keep it, and it is most fit that He should receive it. All things are safe in Jehovah's hands; what we entrust to the Lord will be secure, both now and in that day of days towards which we are hastening. It is peaceful living and glorious dying to repose in the care of Heaven. At all times we should commit our all to Jesus' faithful hand; then, though life may hang on a thread, and adversities may multiply as the sands of the sea, our soul shall dwell at ease, and delight itself in quiet resting places.

NOVEMBER 11.

"The bow shall be seen in the cloud."—Genesis ix. 14.

*W*HEN may we *expect to see the token of the covenant?* The rainbow is only to be seen painted upon a *cloud*. Beloved, our God, who is as the sun to us, always shines, but we do not always see Him—clouds hide His face; but no matter what drops may be falling, or what clouds may be threatening, if *He* does but shine, there will be a rainbow at once. It is said that when we see the rainbow the shower is over. Certain it is, that when Christ comes our troubles remove, when we behold Jesus our sins vanish, and our debts and fears subside. When Jesus walks the waters of the sea, how profound the calm!

NOVEMBER 12.

*T*HE bow shall be in the cloud; and *I* will look upon it, that *I* may remember the everlasting covenant." Oh, it is not *my* remembering God, it is God's remembering *me,* which is the ground of my safety; it is not *my* laying hold of his covenant, but his covenant's laying hold on me. Glory be to God! the whole of the bulwarks of salvation are secured by divine power, and even the minor towers, which we may imagine might have been left to man, are guarded by almighty strength. Even the *remembrance* of the covenant is not left to our memories, for *we* might forget; but our Lord cannot forget the saints whom he has graven on the palms of his hands.

NOVEMBER 13.

*B*EHOLD one of the great Physician's mightiest arts; he has power to forgive sin! Before the ransom had been paid, before the blood had been literally sprinkled on the mercy seat, he had power to forgive sin. Hath he not power to do it now that he hath died? He has boundless power now that he has finished transgression and made an end of sin. Hear him pleading before the eternal Father, pointing to his wounds, urging the merit of his sacred passion! What power to forgive is here! "He is exalted on high to give repentance and remission of sins." The most crimson sins are removed by the crimson of his blood.

NOVEMBER 14.

"And I will give you a heart of flesh."—Ezekiel xxxvi. 26.

*T*HE hard heart does not love the Redeemer, but, the renewed heart burns with affection towards him. Many are the privileges of this renewed heart: " 'Tis here the Spirit dwells, 'tis here that Jesus rests." It is fitted to receive every spiritual blessing, and every blessing comes to it. It is prepared to yield every heavenly fruit to the honor and praise of God, and therefore the Lord delights in it. A tender heart is the best defense against sin, and the best preparation for heaven. A renewed heart stands on its watertower looking for the coming of the Lord Jesus. Have you this heart of flesh?

NOVEMBER 15.

*T*HERE is no elevation of grace, no attainment of spirituality, no clearness of assurance, no post of duty, which is not open to you if you have but the power to believe. Lay aside your sackcloth and ashes, and rise to the dignity of your true position. The golden throne of assurance is waiting for you! The crown of communion with Jesus is ready to bedeck your brow. Wrap yourself in scarlet and fine linen and fare sumptuously every day; if thou believest, thy land shall flow with milk and honey, and thy soul shall be satisfied as with marrow and fatness. Gather golden sheaves of grace, for they await thee in the fields of faith. "All things are possible to him that believeth."

NOVEMBER 16.

"I said not unto the seed of Jacob, Seek ye me in vain."
Isaiah xlv. 19.

*G*OD has clearly revealed that He *will* hear the prayer of those who call upon him, and that declaration cannot be contravened. He was so firmly, so truthfully, so righteously spoken, that there can be no room for doubt. He does not reveal his mind in unintelligible words, but he speaks plainly and positively, "Ask, and ye shall receive." Believe, O trembler, this sure truth—that prayer must and shall be heard, and that never, even in the secrets of eternity, has the Lord said unto any living soul, "Seek ye Me in vain."

NOVEMBER 17.

SINCE the first hour in which goodness came into conflict with evil, it has never ceased to be true in spiritual experience, that Satan hinders us. If we toil in the field, he seeks to break the plough-share; if we build the wall, he labors to cast down the stones; if we would serve God in suffering or in conflict, everywhere Satan hinders us. He hinders us when we are first coming to Jesus Christ. Fierce conflicts we had with Satan when we first looked to the cross and lived. Now that we are saved, he endeavors to hinder the completeness of our personal character. "Let him that thinketh he standeth, take heed lest he fall."

NOVEMBER 18.

AT this moment, dear reader, whatever thy sinfulness, Christ has power to pardon,—power to pardon *thee,* and millions such as thou art. A word will speak it. He has nothing more to do to win thy pardon; all the atoning work is done. He can, in answer to thy tears, forgive thy sins to-day, and make thee know it. He can breathe into thy soul at this very moment a peace with God which passeth all understanding, which shall spring from perfect remission of thy manifold iniquities. Dost thou believe that? I trust thou believest it. Mayst thou experience now the power of Jesus to forgive sin!

NOVEMBER 19.

*B*OUNTEOUS is Jehovah in his nature; to give is his delight. His gifts are beyond measure precious, and are as freely given as the light of the sun. He gives grace to his elect because he wills it, to his redeemed because of his covenant, to the called because of his promise, to believers because they seek it, to sinners because they need it. He gives grace abundantly, seasonably, constantly, readily, sovereignly; doubly enhancing the value of the boon by the manner of its bestowal. Reader, how blessed it is, as the years roll round, and the leaves begin again to fall, to enjoy such an unfading promise as this. "The Lord will give grace."

NOVEMBER 20.

*T*HE dispensation of the old covenant was that of distance. When God appeared even to his servant Moses, he said, "Draw not nigh hither: put off thy shoes from off thy feet;" and when he manifested himself upon Mount Sinai to his own chosen and separated people, one of the first commands was, "Thou shalt set bounds about the mount." When the gospel came, we were placed on quite another footing. The word "Go" was exchanged for "Come," distance was made to give place to nearness, and we who aforetime were afar off, were made nigh by the blood of Jesus Christ. "Come unto Me, all ye that labor and are heavy laden, and I will give you rest."

NOVEMBER 21.

OH, how precious is Christ! How can it be that I have thought so little of him! How is it I can go abroad for joy and comfort when he is so full, so rich, so satisfying? Fellow-believer, make a covenant with thine heart, and ask thy Lord to ratify it. Bid him set thee as a signet upon his finger, and as a bracelet upon his arm. The sparrow hath made a house, and the swallow a nest for herself where she may lay her young, even thine altars, O Lord of hosts, my King and my God; and so too would I make my nest, my home, in thee, and never from thee may the soul of thy turtle dove go forth again, but may I nestle close to thee, O Jesus, my true and only rest.

NOVEMBER 22.

GOD employs his people to encourage one another. We should be glad that God usually works for man by man. It forms a bond of brotherhood, and being mutually dependent on one another, we are fused more completely into one family. Brethren, take the text as God's message to you Aim to comfort the sorrowful, and to animate the desponding. Speak a word in season to him that is weary, and encourage those who are fearful to go on their way with gladness. God encourages you by his promises; Christ encourages *you* as he points to the heaven he has won for you, and the Spirit encourages *you* as he works in you to will and to do of His own will and pleasure.

NOVEMBER 23.

_M_OST of us know what it is to be overwhelmed in heart. Disappointments and heartbreaks will do this when billow after billow rolls over us, and we are like a broken shell hurled to and fro by the surf. Blessed be God, at such seasons we are not without an all-sufficient solace; our God is the harbor of weather-beaten sails, the hospice of forlorn pilgrims. Higher than we are is he, his mercy higher than our sins, his love higher than our thoughts. A rock he is since he changes not, and a high rock, because the tempests which overwhelm us roll far beneath at his feet. O Lord, our God, by thy Holy Spirit, teach us thy way of faith, lead us unto thy rest.

NOVEMBER 24.

_V_ERY bitter is the enmity of the world against the people of Christ. Men will forgive a thousand faults in others, but they will magnify the most trivial offense in the follower of Jesus. Instead of vainly regretting this, let us turn it to account, and since so many are watching for our halting, let this be a special motive for walking very carefully before God. If we live carelessly, the lynx-eyed world will soon see it, and they will shout triumphantly, "See how these Christians act!" The cross of Christ is in itself an offense to the world; let us take heed that we add no offense of our own, for thus can much damage be done to the cause of Christ, and much insult offered to his name.

NOVEMBER 25.

*D*OES Christ receive us when we come to him, notwithstanding all our past sinfulness? Does he never chide us for having tried all other refuges first? And is there none on earth like him? Is he the best of all the good, the fairest of all the fair? Oh, then let us praise him! Daughters of Jerusalem, extol him with timbrel and harp! Now let the standards of pomp and pride be trampled under foot, but let the cross of Jesus, which the world frowns and scoffs at, be lifted on high. Oh for a throne of ivory for our King! Let him be set on high forever, and let my soul sit at his footstool, and kiss his feet, and wash them with my tears.

NOVEMBER 26.

*T*HIS Man receiveth sinners;" not, however, that they may remain sinners, but he receives them that he may pardon their sins, justify their persons, cleanse their hearts by his purifying word, preserve their souls by the indwelling of the Holy Ghost, and enable them to serve him, to show forth his praise, and to have communion with him. Into his heart's love he receives sinners, takes them from darkness, and wears them as jewels in his crown; plucks them as brands from the burning, and preserves them as costly monuments of his mercy. None are so precious in Jesus' sight as the sinners for whom he died.

NOVEMBER 27.

SUCCESS is certain when the Lord has promised it. Although you may have pleaded month after month without evidence of answer, it is not possible that the Lord should be deaf when his people are earnest in a matter which concerns his glory. Delayed answers often set the heart searching itself, and so lead to contrition and spiritual reformation.

Reader, do not fall into the sin of unbelief, but continue in prayer and watching. Plead the precious blood with unceasing importunity, and it shall be with you according to your desire.

NOVEMBER 28.

WE are none of us so much awake as we should be. With a perishing world around us, to sleep is cruel. Oh, that we may leave forever the couch of ease, and go forth with flaming torches to meet the coming Bridegroom! *My heart waketh.* This is a happy sign. Life is not extinct, though sadly smothered. When our renewed heart struggles against our natural heaviness, we should be grateful to sovereign grace for keeping a little vitality within the body of this death. Jesus will hear our hearts, will help our hearts, will visit our hearts; for the voice of the wakeful heart is really the voice of our Beloved, saying, "Open to me." Holy zeal will surely unbar the door.

*I*N *the evening of the day* opportunities are plentiful: men return from their labor, and the zealous soul-winner finds time to tell abroad the love of Jesus. Have I no evening work for Jesus? If I have not, let me no longer withhold my hand from a service which requires abundant labor. Jesus gave both his hands to the nails; how can I keep back one of mine from his blessed work? Night and day he toiled and prayed for me; how can I give a single hour to selfish indulgence? Up, idle heart; stretch out thy hand to work, or uplift it to pray: heaven and hell are in earnest; let me be so, and this evening sow good seed for the Lord my God.

NOVEMBER 30.

"Now on whom dost thou trust."—Isaiah xxxvi. 5.

*R*EADER, this is an important question. Listen to the Christian's answer, and see if it is yours. "On whom dost thou trust?" "I trust," says the Christian, *the Son*—the man Christ Jesus. I trust in him to take away all my sins by his own sacrifice, and to adorn me with his perfect righteousness. I trust him to be my Intercessor, to present my prayers and desires before his Father's throne, and I trust him to be my Advocate at the last great day, to plead my cause, and to justify me. I trust him for what he is, for what he has done, and for what he has promised yet to do

DECEMBER 1.

*T*HIS age is peculiarly the dispensation of the Holy Spirit, in which Jesus cheers us not by his personal presence, as he shall do by and by, but by the indwelling and constant abiding of the Holy Ghost, who is evermore the Comforter of the church. It is his office to console the hearts of God's people. He convinces of sin; he illuminates and instructs; but still the main part of his work lies in making glad the hearts of the renewed, in confirming the weak, and lifting up all those that be bowed down. He does this by revealing Jesus to them. The Holy Spirit consoles, but Christ *is the consolation.*

DECEMBER 2.

*I*S, then, your calling a high calling? Has it ennobled your heart, and set it upon heavenly things? Has it elevated your hopes, your tastes, your desires? If man alone call thee, thou art un-called. Is thy calling of God? Is it a call *to* heaven as well as from heaven? Unless thou art a stranger here, and heaven thy home, thou hast not been called with a heavenly calling; for those who have been so called, declare that they look for a city which hath foundations, whose builder and maker is God. Is thy calling thus holy, high, heavenly? Then, beloved, thou hast been called of God, for such is the calling wherewith God doth call his people.

DECEMBER 3.

*M*ANY in waiting upon the Lord find immediate delight, but this is not the case with all. A deeper sense of sin may be given to you instead of a sense of pardon, and in such a case you will have need of patience to bear the heavy blow. Ah! poor heart, though Christ beat and bruise thee, or even slay thee, trust him; though he should give thee an angry word, believe in the love of his heart. Do not, I beseech thee, give up seeking or trusting my Master because thou hast not yet obtained the conscious joy which thou longest for. Cast thyself on him, and perseveringly depend even where thou canst not rejoicingly hope.

DECEMBER 4.

If any man sin, we have an advocate with the Father, Jesus Christ the righteous."—I John ii. 1.

*W*HAT words of tenderness, what sentences of persuasion, will the anointed use when he stands up to plead for me! "Jesus Christ *the righteous.*" This is not only his character, BUT his plea. It is his character, and if the Righteous One be my advocate, then my cause is good, or he would not have espoused it. It is his plea, for he meets the charge of unrighteousness against me by the plea that *He* is righteous. He declares himself my substitute, and puts his obedience to my account. My soul, thou hast a friend well fitted to be thine advocate; he cannot but succeed; leave thyself entirely in his hands.

DECEMBER 5.

*D*O not dissociate Jesus from our common manhood. It is a dark room which you are going through, but Jesus went through it before. It is a sharp fight which you are waging, but Jesus has stood foot to foot with the same enemy. Let us be of good cheer—Christ has borne the load before us, and the blood-stained footsteps of the King of glory may be seen along the road which we traverse at this hour. There is something sweeter yet— Jesus was tempted, but Jesus never sinned. Then, my soul, it is not needful for thee to sin, for Jesus was a man, and if one man endured these temptations and sinned not, then in his power his members may also cease from sin.

DECEMBER 6.

*W*E shall never sing *Gloria in excelsis* except we pray to God *De profundis:* out of the depths must we cry, or we shall never behold glory in the highest. Prayer should be perfumed with love, saturated with love—love to our fellow-saints, and love to Christ. A man prevails in prayer only as he believes. The Holy Spirit is the author of faith, and strengthens it so that we pray believing God's promise. Oh that this blessed combination of excellent graces, priceless, and sweet as the spices of the merchant, might be fragrant within us because the Holy Ghost is in our hearts! Most blessed Comforter, exert thy mighty power within us, helping our infirmities in prayer.

DECEMBER 7.

And I will deliver thee out of the hand of the wicked, and I will redeem thee out of the hand of the terrible."
—Jer. xv. 21

NOTE the glorious personality of the promise—*I* will, *I* will. The Lord Jehovah himself interposes to deliver and redeem his people. He pledges himself personally to rescue them. His own arm shall do it, that he may have the glory. Neither our strength nor our weakness is taken into the account, but the lone *I*, like the sun in the heavens, shines out resplendent in all-sufficiency. Why then do we calculate our forces, and consult with flesh and blood to our grievous wounding? Peace, ye unbelieving thoughts, be still, and know that the Lord reigneth.

DECEMBER 8.

BE it ever in your remembrance, that to keep strictly in the path of your Saviour's command is better than any outward form of religion; and to hearken to his precept with an attentive ear is better than to bring the fat of rams, or any other precious thing, to lay upon his altar. If you are failing to keep the least of Christ's commands to his disciples, I pray you be disobedient no longer. "To obey," even in the slightest and smallest thing, "is better than sacrifice." It is a blessed thing to be teachable as a little child, but it is a much more blessed thing, when one has been taught the lesson, to carry it out to the letter.

DECEMBER 9.

OUR good Shepherd has in his flock a variety of experiences; some are strong in the Lord, and others are weak in faith; but he is impartial in his care for all his sheep, and the weakest lamb is as dear to him as the most advanced in the flock. Lambs are wont to lag behind, prone to wander, and apt to grow weary; but from all the danger of these infirmities the Shepherd protects them with his arm of power. He finds new-born souls, like your lambs, ready to perish,—he nourishes them till life becomes vigorous; he finds weak minds ready to faint and die—he consoles them and renews their strength.

DECEMBER 10.

THERE are times in our spiritual experience when human counsel or sympathy, or religious ordinances, fail to comfort or help us. Why does our gracious God permit this? Perhaps it is because we have been living too much without him, and he therefore takes away everything upon which we have been in the habit of depending, that he may drive us to himself. It is a blessed thing to live at the fountain head. Having nothing of our own to trust to, but resting upon the merits of Jesus. Beloved, when we are brought to a thirsting condition, we are sure to turn to the fountain of life with eagerness.

DECEMBER 11.

*I*T was a divine song, which Habakkuk sang, when in the night he said, "Although the fig tree shall not blossom, neither shall fruit be in the vines; the labor of the olive shall fail, and the fields shall yield no meat; the flock shall be cut off from the fold, and there shall be no herd in the stalls: yet I will rejoice in the Lord, I will joy in the God of my salvation." No man can make a song in the night of himself; he may attempt it, but he will find that a song in the night must be divinely inspired. O thou chief musician, let us not remain songless because affliction is upon us, tune thou our lips to the melody of thanksgiving.

DECEMBER 12.

*T*HERE are times when all the promises and doctrines of the Bible are of no avail, unless a gracious hand shall apply them to us. To meet this need there is one, even the Spirit of truth, who takes of the things of Jesus, and applies them to us. Think not that Christ hath placed his joys on heavenly shelves that we may climb up to them for ourselves, but he draws near, and sheds his peace abroad in our hearts. O Christian, if thou art to-day laboring under deep distresses, thy Father does not give thee promises and then leave thee to draw them from the word, but the promises he has written in the word he will write anew on your heart.

DECEMBER 13.

GOD says to you, "Fear not, I am thy shield, and thy exceeding great reward." Believer, grasp the divine word with a personal, appropriating faith. Think that you hear Jesus say, "I have prayed for *thee* that thy faith fail not." Think you see him walking on the waters of thy trouble, for he is there, and he is saying, "Fear not, it is I; be not afraid." Oh, those sweet words of Christ! May the Holy Ghost make you feel them as spoken to *you;* forget the others for a while—accept the voice of Jesus as addressed to you, and say, "Jesus whispers consolation; I cannot refuse it; I will sit under his shadow with great delight."

DECEMBER 14.

WHEN is the Christian most liable to sleep? Is it not *when his temporal circumstances are prosperous?* Have you not found it so? When you had daily troubles to take to the throne of grace, were you not more wakeful than you are now? Another dangerous time is *when all goes pleasantly in spiritual matters.* There is no temptation half so dangerous as not being tempted. The distressed soul does not sleep; it is after we enter into peaceful confidence and full assurance that we are in danger of slumbering. The disciples fell asleep after they had seen Jesus transfigured on the mountain top. Take heed, joyous Christian; be as happy as you will, only be watchful.

DECEMBER 15.

*T*O give to others is but sowing seed for ourselves. He who is so good a steward as to be willing to use his substance for his Lord, shall be intrusted with more. Friend of Jesus, art thou rendering him according to the benefit received? Much has been given thee—what is thy fruit? Hast thou done all? Canst thou not do more? To be selfish is to be wicked. God forbid that any of us should follow the ungenerous and destructive policy of living unto ourselves. Jesus pleased not himself. All fullness dwells in him, but of his fullness have we all received. O for Jesus' spirit, that henceforth we may live not unto ourselves!

DECEMBER 16.

But their eyes were holden that they should not know him.
—Luke xxiv. 16.

*T*HE disciples had heard his voice so often, and gazed upon that marred face so frequently, that it is wonderful they did not discover him. Yet is it not so with you also? You have not seen Jesus lately. You have been to his table, and you have not met him there. You are in a dark trouble this day, and though he plainly says, "It is I, be not afraid," yet you cannot discern him. Dear child of God, are you in this state? Faith alone can bring us to see Jesus. Make it your prayer, "Lord, open thou mine eyes, that I may see my Saviour present with me."

DECEMBER 17.

*O*UR Lord would have all his people rich in high and happy thoughts concerning his blessed person. As a help to high thoughts of Christ, remember the estimation that Christ is had in beyond the skies. Think how God esteems the only begotten, his unspeakable gift to us. Consider what the angels think of him, as they count it their highest honor to veil their faces at his feet. Think of the mighty love which drew him from his throne to die upon the cross! See him risen, crowned, glorified! Bow before him as the Wonderful, the Counselor, the mighty God, for only thus will your love to him be what it should.

DECEMBER 18.

O CHRISTIAN, do you doubt as to whether God will fulfill his promise? Shall the munitions of rock be carried by storm? Shall the storehouses of heaven fail? Do you think that your heavenly Father, though he knoweth that you have need of food and raiment, will yet forget you? When not a sparrow falls to the ground without your Father, and the very hairs of your head are all numbered, will you mistrust and doubt him? Full many there be who have been tried till at last they have been driven to exercise faith in God, and the moment of their faith has been the instant of their deliverance.

DECEMBER 19.

*A*RE you willing, dear reader, to receive Christ? then there is no difficulty in the way; Christ will be your guest; his own power is working with you, making you willing. What an honor to entertain the Son of God! The heaven of heavens cannot contain him, and yet he condescends to find a house within our hearts! We are not worthy that he should come under our roof, but what an unutterable privilege when he condescends to enter! for then he makes a feast, and causes us to feast with him upon royal dainties; we sit at a banquet where he gives immortality to those who feed thereon. Blessed among the sons of Adam is he who entertains the Lord.

DECEMBER 20.

*I*N order to learn how to discharge your duty as a witness for Christ, look at His example. He is always witnessing: by the well of Samaria, or in the Temple of Jerusalem: by the lake of Gennesaret, or on the mountain's brow. He witnesses so clearly and distinctly that there is no mistake in Him. Christian, make your life a clear testimony. Be you as the brook wherein you may see every stone at the bottom. You need not say, "I am true;" *be* true. Study your great Exemplar, and be filled with His Spirit. Remember that you need much teaching, much upholding, much grace, and much humility, if your witnessing is to be to your Master's glory.

DECEMBER 21.

*T*HE more you know about Christ, the less will you be satisfied with superficial views of Him; and the more deeply you study His iife and the fullness of His Grace which shines in all His offices, the more truly will you see the King in his beauty. Long more and more to see Jesus. *Meditation and contemplation* are often like windows of agate, and gates of carbuncle, through which we behold the Redeemer. Meditation puts the telescope to the eye, and enables us to see Jesus better than we could have seen him if we had lived in the days of his flesh. Would that we were more taken up with the person, the work, the beauty of our incarnate Lord.

DECEMBER 22.

*I*T is our wisdom, as well as our necessity, to beseech God continually to strengthen that which he has wrought in us. We often forget that the Author of our faith must be the Preserver of it also. The lamp which was burning in the temple was never allowed to go out, but it had to be daily replenished with fresh oil; in like manner, our faith can only live by being sustained with the oil of grace, and we can only obtain this from God himself.

Let us, then, day by day, go to our Lord for the grace and strength we need. We have a strong argument to plead, for it is *his own work of grace* which we ask him to strengthen. Only let your faith take hold of his strength.

DECEMBER 23.

*T*HE distinguishing mark of a Christian is his confidence in the love of Christ, and the yielding of his affections to Christ in return. First, faith sets her seal upon the man by enabling the soul to say with the apostle, "Christ loved me and gave himself for me." Then love gives the countersign, and stamps upon the heart gratitude and love to Jesus in return. "We love him because he first loved us." In those grand old ages, which are the heroic period of the Christian religion, this double mark was clearly to be seen in all believers in Jesus; they were men who knew the love of Christ, and rested upon it as a man leaneth upon a staff whose trustiness he has tried.

DECEMBER 24.

*O*UR heavenly Father often draws us with the cords of love. How slowly do we respond to his gentle impulse! *He draws us to exercise a more simple faith in him;* but we have not yet attained to Abraham's confidence; we do not leave our worldly cares with God. Our meager faith brings leanness into our souls; we do not open our hearts wide, though God has promised to fill them. Does he not this day draw us to trust him? Can we not hear him say, "Come, my child, and trust me. The veil is rent; enter into my presence, I am worthy of thy fullest confidence; cast thy cares on me. Shake thyself from the dust of thy cares, and put on thy beautiful garments of joy."

DECEMBER 25.

*W*E esteem every day alike, but still, as the season suggests thoughts of Jesus, let us joyfully remember our dear Redeemer's glorious birth. Who but He was ever longed for by such a multitude of hearts? When did angels indulge in midnight songs, or did God hang a new star in the sky? To whose cradle did rich and poor make so willing a pilgrimage, and offer such hearty and unsought oblations? Well may earth rejoice; well may all men cease their labor to celebrate "the great birthday" of Jesus. Let gladness rule the hour; let holy song and sweet heart music accompany our soul in the raptures of joy.

DECEMBER 26.

*W*HAT bliss to be a perfectly pardoned soul! My soul dedicates all her powers to Him who, of His own unpurchased love, became my surety, and wrought out for me redemption through His blood! What riches of grace does free forgiveness exhibit! To forgive at all, to forgive fully, to forgive freely, to forgive ever! Here is a constellation of wonders; and when I think of how great my sins were, how dear were the precious drops which cleansed me from them I am in a maze of wondering, worshiping affection. I bow before the throne which absolves me; I clasp the cross which delivers me; I serve henceforth the Incarnate God, through whom I am this day a pardoned soul

DECEMBER 27.

*A*T this hour we rest in the promises of our faithful God, knowing that his words are full of truth and power; we rest in the doctrines of his word, which are consolation itself; we rest in the covenant of his grace, which is a haven of delight. The person of Jesus is the quiet resting place of his people; and when we draw near to him in the breaking of bread, in the hearing of the word, the searching of the Scriptures, prayer, or praise, we find any form of approach to him to be the return of peace to our spirits. The God of Peace gives perfect peace to those whose hearts are stayed upon him.

DECEMBER 28.

*N*OTHING can satisfy the entire man but the Lord's love, and the Lord's own self. To embrace our Lord Jesus, to dwell in His love, and be fully assured of union with Him—this is all in all. Dear reader, you need not try other forms of life in order to see whether they are better than the Christian's: if you roam the world around, you will see no sights like a sight of the Saviour's face; if you could have all the comforts of life, if you lost your Saviour, you would be wretched; but if you win Christ, you would find it a paradise; should you live in obscurity, or die with famine, you will yet be satisfied with favor, and full of the goodness of the Lord.

DECEMBER 29.

*H*IS *presence will be most realized by those who are most like him.* If you desire to see Christ, you must grow in conformity to him. Bring yourself, by the power of the Spirit, into union with Christ's desires, and motives, and plans of action, and you will be in fellowship with him. Remember *his presence may be had.* His promise is as true as ever. He delights to be with us. If he doth not come, it is because we hinder him by our indifference. He will reveal himself to our earnest prayers, and graciously suffer himself to be detained by our entreaties, and by our tears, for these are the golden chains which bind Jesus to his people.

DECEMBER 30.

*C*HRIST appears as a Shepherd to his own sheep, not to others. As soon as he appears, his own sheep perceive him—they trust him, they are prepared to follow him; he knows them, and they know him—there is a mutual knowledge—there is a constant connection between them. Thus the one mark, the sure mark, the infallible mark of regeneration and adoption is a hearty faith in the appointed Redeemer. Reader, are you in doubt, are you uncertain whether you bear the secret mark of God's children? Then let not an hour pass over your head till you have said, "Search me, O God, and know my heart."

DECEMBER 31.

*O*N the last day, that great day of the feast Jesus stood and cried, saying, if any man thirst, let him come unto me *and* drink!" No other distinction is made but that of thirst. No waiting or preparation is so much as hinted at. Drinking represents a reception for which no fitness is required. Sinful lips may touch the stream of divine love, they cannot pollute it, but shall themselves be purified. Jesus is the fount of hope. Dear reader, hear the dear Redeemer's loving voice as he cries to each of us, "If any man thirst, let him come unto me and drink."